VOLUME 29

MARTIN
B-26 MARAUDER

BY FREDERICK A. JOHNSEN

specialty press
PUBLISHERS AND WHOLESALERS

Published by
Specialty Press Publishers and Wholesalers
11605 Kost Dam Road
North Branch, MN 55056
United States of America
(651) 583-3239

Distributed in the UK and Europe by
Airlife Publishing Ltd.
101 Longden Road
Shrewsbury
SY3 9EB
England

ISBN 1-58007-029-9

Designed by Dennis R. Jenkins

Printed in the United States of America

Front Cover: *Kermit Weeks' short-wing B-26 was photographed in 1998 over Florida. This Marauder missed combat when it was forced down in the wilderness on its delivery flight to Alaska in January 1942. Its initial recovery and restoration were undertaken by David Tallichet's warbird organization. Aero Trader subsequently worked on the rare B-26 for Kermit Weeks. (Copyrighted photo by Jim Koepnick courtesy Experimental Aircraft Association)*
Back Cover (Left Top): *A Martin employee worked on a Marauder tail gun mount which used the Bell M-6 boosted hydraulic unit introduced during B-model production. (Martin via Stan Piet)*
Back Cover (Right Top): *A gleaming cutaway Pratt & Whitney R-2800-5 engine was a training aid at the Martin B-26 school. (AFHRA)*
Back Cover (Lower): *Forward Fuselage structure of the B-26. (Frederick A. Johnsen Collection)*

TABLE OF CONTENTS

THE MARTIN B-26 MARAUDER

PREFACE

AND THE THANKS GO TO ...

The Martin B-26 Marauder occupies a controversial place on the bookshelf of some enthusiasts and historians. In its early iterations, the Marauder exhibited traits that were sometimes hazardous to neophyte bomber pilots. Some wags called the B-26 the *Separator*, because its handling idiosyncrasies separated the men from the boys. Yet, as all too often happens, the negative stories have lingered long after the B-26 evolved into a viable weapon in the arsenal of the Army Air Forces. By late 1943, stories of crews deplaning from a Marauder and checking the sides of the fuselage for silver casket handles were couched in the past tense.

There's a recurring theme in the Marauder's procurement and development — a theme that still plays in aircraft acquisition programs more than six decades later. In an effort to streamline the flow of the promising B-26 Marauder into the AAF, it was procured as the first in a series of "off-the-shelf" programs, with compressed development times to hasten production.

Nonetheless, military aircraft programs — at least those which endeavor to push back the frontiers of technology in a meaningful way by introducing new ideas — must be nurtured through sometimes-trying developmental periods. The Marauder had to endure development work even after it was ordered into production, as early models revealed deficiencies only made worse by evolving combat needs.

This look at the Martin Marauder gets under the B-26's skin, with references to technical manuals and official Army Air Forces reports and wartime correspondence. As with any book of this nature, the final result was boosted by the help of many people and institutions, including: Air Force Historical Research Agency (AFHRA), Laurent Boulestin, Peter M. Bowers, Don Keller, Cam Martin, Bill Miranda, San Diego Aerospace Museum, and Carl Scholl (Aero Trader). Special thanks to Tom Poberezny, Sue Smick, and photographer Jim Koepnick of the Experimental Aircraft Association for the loan of Koepnick's inflight photo of Kermit Weeks' Marauder.

Somebody else deserves thanks for helping this book get to press: You. Thank you for buying this volume in the *WarbirdTech* series. You have made possible the phenomenal growth of this series since its inception in 1996. I am mindful of that, and promise to do my best to uncover new and interesting facts and artwork to hold your interest.

Abbreviations used in notes and photo captions include AFHRA (Air Force Historical Research Agency, Maxwell AFB, Alabama) and SDAM (San Diego Aerospace Museum).

Frederick A. Johnsen
March 2000

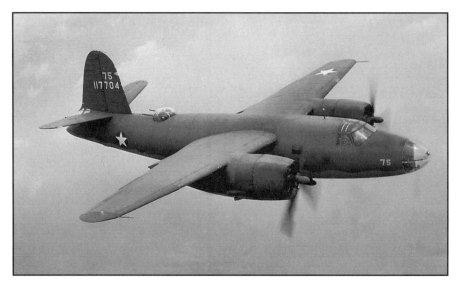

Short tail version of B-26B (41-17704) was photographed for general AAF identification purposes. (Larkins via Bowers)

MAKING THE MARAUDER

The Martin B-26 Marauder represented an experiment in procurement by the U.S. Army Air Corps. It was the first of several aircraft for which contracts were issued based on drawing board plans instead of flying prototypes. This process, called off-the-shelf procurement, netted the Glenn L. Martin Company a contract for 201 examples of its proposed Model 179, a twin-engine bomber, based on the company's winning response to Circular Proposal 39-640, issued on 11 March 1939.[1]

In the post–Cold War 1990s, American aircraft manufacturing was characterized by a series of buy-outs and mergers that limited the surviving conglomerates

to a handful of prime contractors — a far cry from the 86 bids invited for consideration under Circular 39-640 in March 1939. Even though that many bidders were invited, only seven bids were received by the U.S. Army Air Corps. Based on a rating system of points, Martin came in first, followed by North American Aviation, Douglas, and Stearman.

Early concepts for the Model 179 called for a twin tail. By October 1939, Martin and Air Corps engineers analyzing test evidence concluded that a single fin and rudder, complemented with horizontal stabilizers with marked dihedral or upsweep, would give better flying characteristics.[2]

By November 1939, an Air Corps board inspected the mock-up of the Martin Model 179 bomber, designated B-26. Already, the "off-the-shelf" design came in for changes, as the mock-up board recommended additions including waist guns. A year later, on 29 November 1940, the B-26 flew for the first time.[3] Even while service pilots were evaluating the first Marauder, Martin was filling its shop floor with follow-on airframes.[4]

Early performance measurements were sufficiently encouraging to warrant its acceptance on 8 February 1941. The service ceiling was 25,000 feet and the absolute ceiling an additional 1,200 feet higher, although typical bombing

The original Marauder was photographed in December 1940. It pioneered use of Martin's own top turret design that became a standard on many warplanes. Lack of anti-glare panel ahead of windscreen would be changed on late production bare metal B-26s. (AAF via Bowers)

altitudes for the Marauder at war would be far less. At 14,250 feet, the B-26 showed its high speed of 323 miles an hour. It had a guaranteed operating speed of 266 miles an hour at 15,000 feet. To achieve a range of 3,000 miles at 15,000 feet, the B-26 burned 1,270 gallons of gasoline. One adverse notation was an "aerodynamic overbalance of the rudder."[5]

The evident folly of "off-the-shelf" procurement showed itself again; a Materiel Command case study of the Martin B-26 program noted: "No sooner was the B-26 accepted than studies were conducted for the purpose of recommending revisions in the airplane." These studies went as far as suggesting incorporation of a pressurized cabin, a seemingly out-of-place feature for a medium bomber of the era. More significant was the call for a new and enlarged wing for the B-26, a topic studied in the first half of 1941.

In July 1941, Brig. Gen. Oliver Echols, chief of the AAF's Materiel

Division, wrote to the chief of the Air Corps: "There is a good deal of difference of opinion as to what is wrong with this airplane. One school of thought is that the present airplane is deficient due to the large amount of resistance resulting from the landing gear doors while open and the stall characteristics which have resulted from the drag in the center section resulting from an effort to cure stall characteristics by placing a spoiler on the leading edge. The second school of thought is that the airplane definitely does not have enough wing area for the present gross weight of the airplane."[6] The issue of wing size ultimately led to a Martin redesign.

The enlarged wing, with span increased to 71 feet from 65 feet, appeared on the 982nd B-26 (the first B-26B-10, sometimes also listed as Block 1) delivered from Martin's Baltimore, Maryland plant. The first aircraft delivered from Martin's other assembly plant in Omaha, Nebraska, was a

big-wing B-26C.[7] In September 1941, as automotive companies were being worked into aircraft production plans, Brig. Gen. George C. Kenney (who would later lead Fifth Air Force including a contingent of B-26s) was assistant chief of the Materiel Division and was involved in the procurement and evolution of the aircraft. On 5 September 1941, he instructed others in the command to: "Tell Martin to put [a] 71 foot wing on automotive B-26 and as soon as possible on B-26s built at Baltimore."[8]

The enlarged wing was accompanied by redesigned bigger tail surfaces. An 8 July 1941 Materiel Division memorandum stated the proposed redesigns of wing and tail, along with fuselage reinforcing and landing gear review, would amount to a 50 percent new aircraft. During this redesign time, as the AAF criticized B-26 takeoff performance, particularly from sod runways, Martin requested the service work to expedite getting versions of the R-2800 engine available for the B-26 with 2000 horsepower for takeoff rating instead of the then-current 1850 horsepower.[9]

While alterations were being pondered and accepted or rejected in the spring of 1941, the B-26s extant were grounded on 21 April

B-26 production line made a sharp u-turn as workers kept the Marauders flowing into service. Much World War II aircraft construction was an accommodation between mass production techniques when feasible and hand-fitting of parts where necessary. (Martin via Bowers)

Early short-wing B-26B in flight shows why wags called the Marauder the flying prostitute, because it had "no visible means of support." (AAF via Bowers)

1941 following nosegear failures ultimately corrected by a change in manufacturing processes including heat treating. A second round of B-26 landing gear malfunctions that September was traced to hydraulic leaks. Ultimately, changes in instructional procedures and larger fluid reservoirs helped ease the problem.

In the summer of 1941 as the need for a bigger wing was being solidified, results of evaluations at Wright Field indicated, according to an AAF B-26 historical summary, "landing and takeoff characteristics of [the] B-26 were disappointing although it was a fairly good plane in the air. The plane could be landed satisfactorily by experienced pilots when

Camouflaged B-26 (no suffix model letter) paused at Boeing Field near Seattle, Washington, late in 1941. Large, highly-visible insignia beneath top turret was superceded with smaller star moved aft, possibly to the relief of top turret gunners. (Gordon S. Williams via Peter M. Bowers)

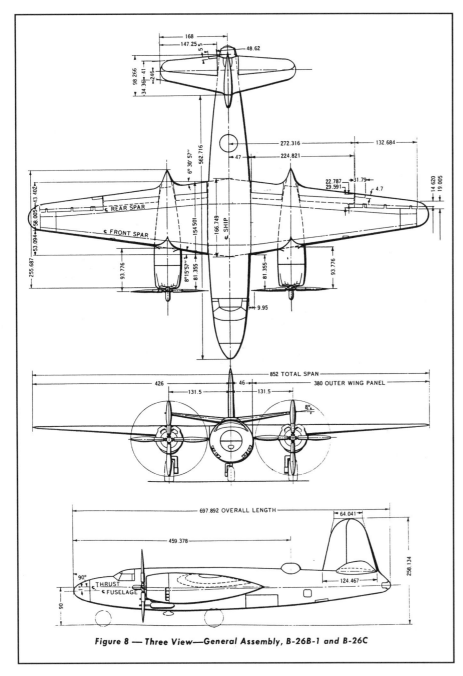

Figure 8 — Three View—General Assembly, B-26B-1 and B-26C

this period one B-26 was winterized at Wright Field, intended as a model for reworking others. On 24 November 1941, Wright Field engineers declared the need for equipping B-26B and C-models to carry torpedoes. Marauders would try torpedoes in the frantic Battle of Midway only seven months later.[11]

Problems with Curtiss Electric propellers on Marauders might be correctable through "standardized technique for ground checking and thorough instruction of maintenance personnel," according to a December 1941 Wright Field engineering report. The Curtiss propeller was described in an AAF history of the B-26 as being "a more complex propeller than a hydraulic type and required a large number of electrical connections, mechanical parts, joints, etc., which could cause operational failure." To help ensure reliable operation of the propellers, Curtiss offered to school AAF personnel in maintenance procedures.[12] (The Curtiss Electric propeller harnessed power for a variety of American warplanes including B-26s, P-38s, many P-39s, P-40s, a lot of P-47s; and many Wildcats, among them. The propellers' evident viability

the proper amount of weight was carried in the tail. However, due to its rate of deceleration, an experienced pilot, who understood its peculiar characteristics, was needed to fly the plane to make a satisfactory landing."[10] This pre-war evaluation possibly contributed to the Marauder's early reputation as being too hot for new crews.

Into the fall of 1941, the AAF and

Martin worked on ironing out bugs in the Marauder's hydraulic system that sometimes resulted in low fluid levels and system malfunctions. Meanwhile, in early November of that year, Wright Field's production engineering section said accelerated service testing of the extant B-26s was disorganized and lacking continuity because of the mechanical problems encountered and the need for training aircrews. During

nonetheless was sometimes overshadowed by occasional problems.)

The mammoth task of converting from peacetime to protracted wartime production of B-26s at Baltimore as well as a second plant at Omaha, Nebraska led to supply bottlenecks that were blamed in March 1942 for keeping about 70 Marauders languishing at the Omaha Modification Center for lack of parts.[13] (Delivery lags were not unique to the Marauder; other warplanes including the Douglas A-26 Invader, early Ford-built B-24Es, and even the vaunted B-29 Superfortress would take their turns at overcoming production hurdles.) By mid-May 1942, the Nebraska Martin plant modification center held about 185 B-26s awaiting changes; what started out as an "off-the-shelf" procurement was now mired deep in developmental issues. During 1942, Martin dramatically increased employment at the Nebraska facility to reduce the modification backlog as well as to train for impending production of C-models.[14]

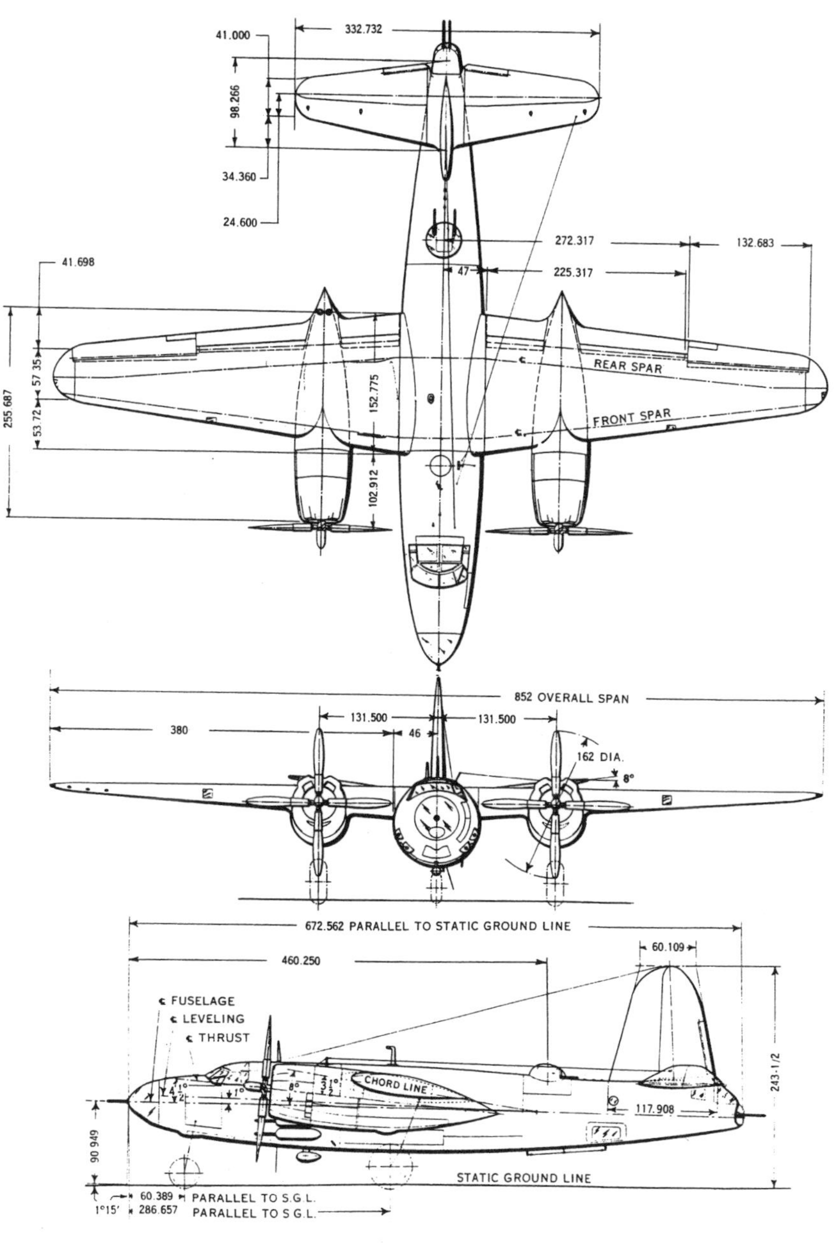

Other problems occasionally arose, and a report sent to Gen. H. H. Arnold, Chief of the Army Air Forces, described the B-26 as a "highly developed, probably over engineered airplane, utilizing many electrical features." On 2 April 1942, Maj. Gen. Carl Spaatz convened a board of officers at Wright Field to investigate the B-26 to determine and report on: 1. the extent the B-26 series was tactically operational; 2. the modifications necessary to make the series operational; 3. provisions for correcting difficulties already experienced; 4. the level

Figure 9 — Three View—General Assembly, B-26F and B-26G

of flying experience required of B-26 pilots; 5. the type of aircraft needed to bridge the training gap between the single-engine AT-6 and the B-26; 6. the degree to which the Marauder series could be considered suitable for tactical operation outside the continental United States; and 7. recommendations regarding continuing production of the B-26 series.[15]

General Spaatz's board met for

four days and developed a list of change recommendations ranging from items the board considered important for safety, to items the board believed vital to making the B-26 tactically suitable, to suggestions to facilitate maintaining and operating the aircraft. The board decided that, as of early April 1942, the B-26 series could not be considered operationally satisfactory without implementation of the board's

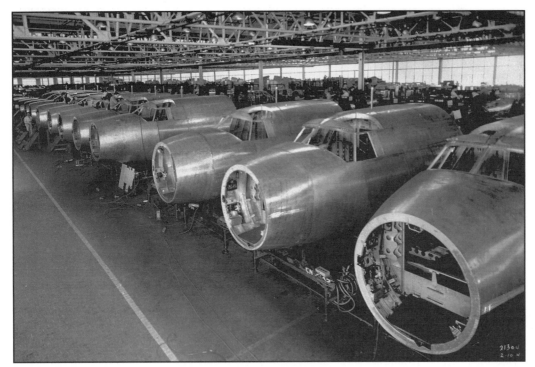

Sectional construction of Marauders also allowed them to be disassembled for shipment if necessary. (AFHRA)

recommendations. Even with such reservations, the board said the Martin B-26 should remain in production.

In early 1941, Martin was directed to seek subcontractors to help with B-26 production and contemplated Chrysler, Goodyear, and the Hudson Motor Car Company. Around this time, the Martin Omaha facility was established, and later this plant obtained the services of the J. I. Case Company to build B-26 wings. In the first few months of 1942, the AAF expressed concern about B-26 production schedules at the Omaha facility. That year, the AAF also contemplated the future of bombardment aviation. The Douglas A-26 Invader was seen as the eventual replacement for both the B-26 Marauder and the North American B-25 Mitchell.[16]

During the first week of October 1942, the AAF's director of military requirements, Maj. Gen. Muir

S. Fairchild, told Gen. Oliver Echols of Materiel Command that the Martin B-26, as a medium bomber, did not fit into classic categories of high-level bombers, low-level bombers, or dive bombers. One possible category was low-level bombing, although Marauders sometimes paid dearly for minimum altitude sorties. General Fairchild, mindful of the recurring question of whether Marauder production should be terminated, recommended making tentative plans for weeding out Marauder production in the event of further problems with the B-26.[17] (Ironically, teething problems with the new Douglas A-26 Invader would delay the time-table by which the Invader could be expected to replace the Marauder.)

In May 1943, Maj. Gen. James H. Doolittle wrote to General Arnold, saying that B-26s and B-25s had done excellent work in North Africa, but their accuracy was less and their losses per sortie more

than the comparable statistics for heavy bombers. General Doolittle elaborated on his view of the bomber force of the near future, describing a force of heavy bombers of the B-29 category, relegating B-17 and B-24 types to medium bomber status, with A-26s as light bombers, all protected by sufficient escort fighters.[18]

In the month following General Doolittle's comments about the composition of the future AAF bomber force, General Arnold requested a committee to consider eliminating the Martin B-26 from production. Recommendations arising from this committee included closing out B-26 construction at Omaha as soon as B-29 production could be started there, and winding down B-26 production at Baltimore to a ceiling of 150 aircraft per month, wrapping it up as soon as anticipated Northrop B-35 Flying Wing production could take its place. The continued

Early prewar photos of American assembly lines often show a nonchalance that quickly dissipated with the demands of combat. Short-wing Marauders, their rudders already painted red, white, and blue, neared completion in the Maryland plant. (Martin/AFHRA)

production of Marauders at Baltimore, according to an AAF study, "was based upon a desire for insuring continuity at the Martin-Baltimore facility throughout the year 1944."[19]

In September 1942, further studies urged weight reduction and redistribution to improve B-26 performance. Typical of aircraft programs, the B-26 had put on weight; nearly a ton would have to be shed to return to the design gross weight of 31,500 pounds, which was already over the initial overload weight of about 29,000 pounds. The inevitable addition of armor plate, leakproof tanks, more guns, ammunition, and radio gear prompted an increase of normal weight to 29,000 pounds, and overload weight to about 31,000 pounds. Still the weight piled on, and in February 1943, the Director of Military Requirements listed items to be deleted from B-26s, including astrodomes, astrographs, astrocompasses, outlets for electrical-

ly-heated flying clothing, and the K-3B camera mount. Big wing B-26s had a maximum weight of 38,200 pounds specified by 19 June 1943.[20]

Leaping into Production

A Martin engineer described the first Marauder as a production aircraft, saying there was no prototype. Martin designers, upon receiving the contract to build the first Marauder, decided the world situation warranted gearing up for quantity production of B-26s right away. Martin officials also presumed their bombers would have to be built by a newly-recruited corps of workers with little previous aircraft experience, making simplicity a virtue.[21]

To accomplish this, the B-26 was created as about 650 minor subassemblies which went into 32 major subassemblies, and thence into a finished Marauder. Frames and stringers were pre-drilled in jigs so they would align for rivet-

ing when brought together in a steel assembly fixture on the shop floor. The streamlined cigar shape of the Marauder resulted in the use of 63 pieces of skin with compound curvatures. A stretch press made these with a high degree of uniformity, saving much time over individual fitting methods for compound-curve metal sheets.[22]

Martin officials planned with a milling machine manufacturer to develop a traveling head mill with a 30-foot bed to cut wing parts with great accuracy. Fixtures for assembling all the parts of a Marauder wing were engineered to be foolproof, so that the parts could only be installed the correct way.[23]

The Sum of Its Parts

Rushing to build 12-ton B-26Cs by committee, the consortium of Martin-Nebraska, Martin-Baltimore, Goodyear, Chrysler, and Hudson experienced problems

Natural metal B-26B (42-96163) of the 397th Bomb Group photographed from the side shows position of engine nacelles and thrust line parallel to fuselage, instead of canting upward as on F- and G-models. (AAF)

and delays during 1942 as changes to the wings beset Goodyear with challenges, and parts from other vendors needed rework at the Martin plant before they could be used. Chrysler tended to be ahead of schedule on delivery of components, but the changes required before those parts could be installed, due to evolving needs, prompted the AAF to have Chrysler do the changes in its plant before shipping the parts to Martin-Nebraska, thereby freeing up Martin for other assembly tasks. Goodyear, who earned a good reputation during the war for building FG-1D variants of the Corsair fighter, initially faced problems with its delivery of viable wings for B-26Cs, a problem blamed in part on the many engineering changes visited upon Marauder wings. In an effort to help Goodyear, the wing design was frozen at a point chosen by Martin to enable Goodyear to deliver a product free of evolving changes; in September 1942, the production engineering section at Wright Field called for selecting an alternate source for B-26 wings and control surfaces to help Goodyear if production requirements exceeded 100 aircraft per month.[24]

In the first half of 1943, C-model Marauders of the 323rd Bomb Group were subjected to a weight reduction test which included removal of the copilot, along with his seat, controls, and some armor plate and the liaison radio set. A howl of protest led to the return of these items to the Group's B-26Cs, thus ending the weight-reduction test.

By June of 1943, AAF chief Gen. Henry H. Arnold expressed his opinion that the variety of some AAF aircraft should be winnowed down, and that both B-25s and B-26s should be phased out of production. General Arnold's observations were influenced at least in part by opinions of some theater commanders that there was no place for medium bombers. If combat conditions were harsh on mediums, another factor loomed large: Figures were circulated that indicated it took 28,900 man-hours to build a B-26 and 33,000 to build a four-engine B-17, with the implication that the

Martin busied itself with production of the B-26 Marauder, photographed in front of an unfinished Model 167 "Maryland" tailwheeled bomber for the RAF, and a PBM Mariner seaplane for the U.S. Navy at the Baltimore factory. (Martin/AFHRA)

WARBIRDTECH
S E R I E S

combat utility of the B-17 returned more on its investment.[25]

Even as the AAF was pondering the phaseout of B-26 production, in July 1943 an idea surfaced in AAF circles that suggested using available B-26s as bomber escorts for B-17 and B-24 formations over Europe. This came after Eighth Air Force B-26s had received a severe drubbing in low-level operations over the Continent. According to a Materiel Command history of the Marauder: "If possible, this would supply a profitable use for B-26s which were available in large numbers and it would solve high rate of losses being suffered in bombardment operations in Europe. B-26s, as escorts, would run interference for the 'bomber elements' and would use both fixed and flexible guns as armament." With an intended gross weight of 35,141 pounds, such a gunship Marauder was forecast to have a top speed of 236 miles an hour at 22,000 feet and a range of 1,550 miles at that altitude if a constant true airspeed of 233 miles an hour was kept.[26] But the scheme of using heavily-gunned bombers to escort other bombers withered in the face of increasingly-capable escort fighters.

The plan to change the angle of incidence of Marauder wings to improve performance was a Martin plan enthusiastically presented to the AAF by the fall of 1943, and embraced for inclusion in Baltimore-built models to be known as B-26Fs and B-26Gs. When the company's request to introduce the new wing incidence initially was declined, Glenn L. Martin visited General Arnold to take up the cause. Martin offered to make the change on new pro-

With the wheel and tire assembly removed for servicing, the right main strut of AT-23A (42-43409) shows the characteristic forward sweep of the Marauder series. The mechanics were servicing the aircraft for the 12th Tow Target Squadron in California in the spring of 1944. (AAF)

As Marauder production expanded, these B-26 bomb bay door assemblies were stockpiled in an Omaha, Nebraska warehouse pending use. (U.S. Army Signal Corps)

duction Marauders at no cost to the government. By early November 1943, Martin received the AAF's directive to make the wing incidence change.[27]

As 1943 wore on, requirements for B-26s diminished. Many were converted to target tugs for the U.S. Navy and the AAF, but some were accumulating at the Martin Nebraska plant, a situation called "demoralizing to Martin workers."[28]

By the first quarter of calendar year 1944, the Glenn L. Martin Company was engaged in production of B-26 Marauders, PBM Mariner seaplanes, A-30 Baltimore twin engine bombers, and the 200-foot wingspan Mars flying boats, as well as power-operated gun turrets for its own as well as other manufacturers' bombers.[29] The Nebraska plant's Marauder adventure was limited to C-models; all models except the B-26C were built by Martin at Baltimore, Maryland.

By the Numbers

With 5,157 Marauders produced by Martin at Baltimore and Omaha, unit cost might be expected to vary with volume and equipment installed. The price of a Marauder was reported by the AAF to be:

1939 – 1941	$261,062
1942	$239,655
1943	$212,932
1944	$192,427

This compared with B-25 prices that were consistently lower, while the Douglas A-26, viewed as an eventual replacement for both the B-25 and B-26, hovered at a unit price comparable to that of the Marauder. In 1943, the AAF said a B-25 could be bought for

When its wingspan was increased, the Marauder lost some of the epithets hurled at it early in its career. Inside upper quarters of engine nacelles had anti-glare paint on natural-metal examples. (AAF)

$151,894, while the A-26 was the high item at $254,624. By comparison, a four-engine heavy Consolidated B-24 Liberator was pegged at $215,516 in 1944, a year during which five assembly lines cranked out Liberators *en masse*, making the B-24 Liberator the most produced American military aircraft of all time.[30]

When war broke out in December 1941, the AAF had about 150 B-26s on hand, albeit not that many were combat-worthy examples. The tally crept upward throughout 1942, with 331 B-26s listed by the end of June, and 712 by the end of the year. The on-hand Marauder tally in the AAF broke 1,000 for the first time by the end of April 1943, when 1,114 B-26s were counted. Peak availability of Marauders in the AAF was put at 1,931 aircraft at the end of March 1944. This dropped to 730 B-26s by the end of August 1945 as Douglas A-26 Invaders continued to replace Martin B-26 Marauders.[31]

[1] *Case History of B-26 Airplane Project,* Air Force Materiel Command History Office, 22 February 1945. [2] *Ibid.* [3] *Ibid.* [4] News release, Martin Co., circa 21 March 1941. [5] *Ibid.* [6] Memorandum for Chief of the Air Corps, Subject: "Discussion with the Martin Company in Regard to Improving Landing and Take-Off Characteristics of the B-26 Airplane," Brig. Gen. Oliver Echols, 2 July 1941. [7] News release, Martin Co., circa 21 March 1941. [8] Memo, Brig. Gen. George C. Kenney to Major Harmon, 5 September 1941. [9] Memorandum Report, Subject: "Experimental program Martin B-26 airplane to improve landing and take-off characteristics," Air Corps Materiel Division, 8 July 1941. [10] *Case History of B-26 Airplane Project,* Air Force Materiel Command History Office, 22 February 1945. [11] *Ibid.* [12] *Ibid.* [13] *Ibid.* [14] *Ibid.* [15] News release, Martin Co., circa 21 March 1941. [16] *Ibid.* [17] *Case History of B-26 Airplane Project,* Air Force Materiel Command History Office, 22 February 1945. [18] *Ibid.* [19] *Ibid.* [20] *Ibid.* [21] Harry F. Kniesche, "Production of Martin B-26 Medium Bombers," *Aero Digest,* April 1941. [22] *Ibid.* [23] *Ibid.* [24] *Case History of B-26 Airplane Project,* Air Force Materiel Command History Office, 22 February 1945. [25] *Ibid.* [26] *Ibid.* [27] *Ibid.* [28] *Ibid.* [29] Howard Mingos, Editor, *The Aircraft Yearbook for 1944,* Lanciar Publishers Inc., New York, New York, 1944. [30] *Army Air Forces Statistical Digest, World War II,* Office of Statistical Control, HQ, USAAF, December 1945. [31] *Ibid.*

Staggered twin rows of cylinders were cut away to show new Marauder crews how their bombers' R-2800 engines operated. Propeller shaft is in the right of the photo. (AAF)

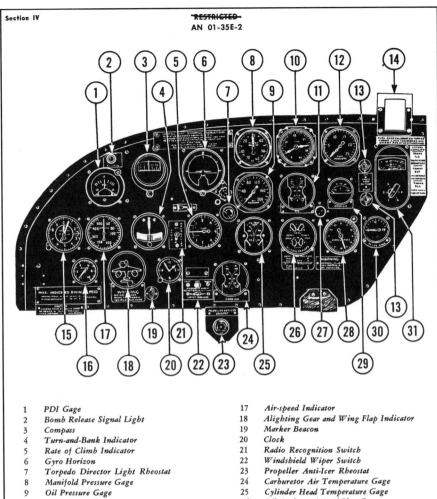

Instruments typically faced by the pilot of the B-26B-1 and B-26C were depicted in the Marauder erection and maintenance manual, commonly called the "Dash-2" book. (Frederick A. Johnsen Collection)

1	PDI Gage	17	Air-speed Indicator
2	Bomb Release Signal Light	18	Alighting Gear and Wing Flap Indicator
3	Compass	19	Marker Beacon
4	Turn-and-Bank Indicator	20	Clock
5	Rate of Climb Indicator	21	Radio Recognition Switch
6	Gyro Horizon	22	Windshield Wiper Switch
7	Torpedo Director Light Rheostat	23	Propeller Anti-Icer Rheostat
8	Manifold Pressure Gage	24	Carburetor Air Temperature Gage
9	Oil Pressure Gage	25	Cylinder Head Temperature Gage
10	RPM Gage (Tachometer)	26	Oil Cooler and Cowl Flap Gage
11	Oil Temperature Gage	27	Torpedo Plug-in
12	Fuel Pressure Gage	28	Radio Compass
13	Propeller Check Switches	29	Free Air Temperature Gage
14	Compass Correction Card	30	De-Icer Gage
15	Altimeter	31	Fuel Gage
16	Suction Gage		

Figure 308 — Pilot's Instrument Panel B-26B-1 and B-26C

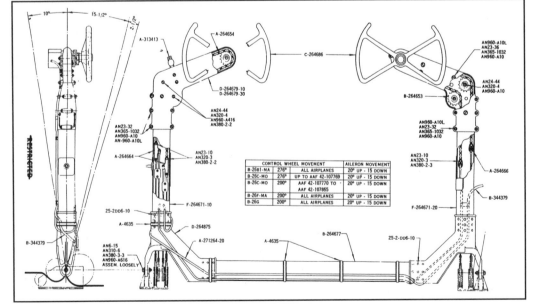

CONTROL WHEEL MOVEMENT		AILERON MOVEMENT
B-26I-MA	276°	ALL AIRPLANES	20° UP - 15 DOWN
B-26C-MO	276°	UP TO AAF 42-107769	20° UP - 15 DOWN
B-26C-MO	200°	AAF 42-107770 TO AAF 42-107855	20° UP - 15 DOWN
B-26F-MA	200°	ALL AIRPLANES	20° UP - 15 DOWN
B-26G	200°	ALL AIRPLANES	20° UP - 15 DOWN

Marauder control wheels were mounted to columns connected by a circular tube at the bottom. The throw of the wheels was rigged for 20 degrees up aileron and 15 degrees down. (Frederick A. Johnsen Collection)

WARBIRDTECH
SERIES

World War II aircraft often underwent instrument layout revisions. This depiction of a typical B-26F and B-26G panel layout shows variations from B- and C-model panels. (Frederick A. Johnsen Collection)

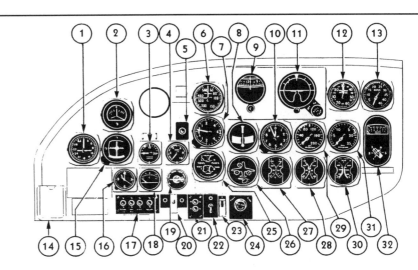

1	Radio Compass	18	Free Air Temperature Indicator
2	Pilot Director	19	Gunsight Rheostat
3	De-Icer Gage	20	Bomb Selector Switch
4	Suction Gage	21	Propeller Switch
5	Marker Beacon	22	Radio Recognition Switch
6	Air-speed Indicator	23	Emergency Control Switch for SCR-695
7	Rate of Climb Indicator	24	Propeller Anti-Icer Rheostat
8	Bank-and-Turn Indicator	25	Cowl Flaps and Oil Cooler Flap Position Indicator
9	Directional Gyro		
10	Altimeter	26	Flaps and Alighting Gear
11	Flight Indicator	27	Carburetor Air Temperature
12	Manifold Pressure Gage	28	Oil Temperature Gage
13	RPM Gage Tachometer	29	Oil Pressure Gage
14	Compass Correction Card Holder	30	Cylinder Head Temperature Gage
15	Radio Indicator	31	Fuel Pressure Gage
16	Clock	32	Fuel Level Gage
17	Bomb and Door Indicator		

Figure 309 — Pilot's Instrument Panel B-26F and B-26G

A Martin training aid was this Marauder bomb bay bulkhead at station 346-1/4. Oval hatch allowed movement of aircrew fore and aft. (Frederick A. Johnsen Collection)

A makeshift wartime scrapyard in Italy held the carcasses of British and American aircraft including the fuselage of a B-26 lying on its side, bottom center. The large circular opening toward the right of the fuselage once accommodated the Martin top turret; the smaller circular opening was for the astrodome hatch. The removal of skin panels from the back of the Marauder wreck reveals stringers and longerons like fish bones. (AAF)

B-26B 41-31879, coded KX-W of the 387th Bomb Group's 558th Bomb Squadron, played out its life on 5 February 1944 (the photo has an alternative style of date marking). A forced landing at Friston, England during its sixth mission resulted in the bomber flinging engines and wrenching its fuselage in a grassy slide. This Marauder was little more than a month in service before its washout, having flown its first mission on 30 December 1943. The Group's tail identifier was a horizontal band with yellow and black diagonal stripes. (Stuart H. Perrin family via Cam Martin)

If the B-26 Marauder needed development even after it was in production, the evolution never broke the mold; the last Marauder built looked very much like the direct descendant of the first B-26 to test its silver wings. And yet salient changes were made.

B-26

In keeping with the premise of an off-the-shelf buy, Marauders began with the straight B-26 designation, bypassing traditional XB and YB test nomenclature. Procurement of B-26s (without a suffix model letter) totaled 201 aircraft. Martin's chief engineer at the time, William K. Ebel, also doubled as pilot on the first flight of a B-26 in November 1940. The R-2800-5 engines of the 201 B-26s

were rated at 1,850 horsepower that could propel the bomber at a high speed of 315 miles an hour. Designer Peyton Magruder gave the early B-26 models a short wingspan of 65 feet — good for fast speeds, but unforgiving at the low end of the Marauder's flying range. Length of the B-26 model was 56 feet. The empty weight of 21,375 pounds could grow to a gross weight of 32,000 pounds. Cruising speed was a brisk 265 miles an hour; range was 1,000 miles. These early B-26s were designed for three .50-caliber and two .30-caliber machine guns plus a bomb load of up to 4,800 pounds.[1]

B-26A

One-hundred-thirty-nine A-models were completed, having a

gross weight 200 pounds heavier than that of the straight B-26s, with the addition of more gasoline tankage in the bomb bay, torpedo carriage provisions, and .50-caliber machine guns in the nose and tail. A change in the electrical system saw B-26As receive the standard military 24-volt system instead of the earlier B-26s' 12-volt system. Most A-models flew with R-2800-9 or -39 engines. B-26As saw combat in 1942 out of Australia with the 22nd Bomb Group, as well as at Midway and in the Aleutians that year.[2]

B-26B

The B-model introduced twin .50-caliber tail guns where previous Marauders had used only one gun. Starting with Dash-5 engines of 1,850 horsepower, B-models

Early B-26 (with no suffix model letter) was photographed at Wright Field. Rushed to production, the Marauder's configuration would evolve later with larger span and increased wing angle of incidence being most noticeable. (AAF via Bowers)

soon were switched to the Dash-41 or -43 powerplant which could give 1,920 horsepower. The B-model started with a .30-caliber tunnel gun for ventral protection, graduating to two low-mounted waist windows offering protection with a .50-caliber gun in each window. In the B-26B-4, an effort was made to improve takeoff performance by increasing the length of the nosewheel strut, resulting in a change of wing angle of incidence during the takeoff run. Slotted flaps made their appearance on Block-5 B-models. Variously identified as Block 1 or Block 10 B-models introduced a significant change to the Marauder line by utilizing bigger wings spanning 71 feet and reducing wing loading for improved low-speed handling.[3]

In July 1942, the production division at Wright Field tallied hundreds of B-26B-1 variants with Dash-43 engines, larger wings, wheels, and tires than earlier B-26Bs.[4]

The B-model could top out at about 317 miles an hour, and cruised at 260. Weight was up several thousand pounds during the development of the B-model series with the addition of bigger wings, four package guns on the forward fuselage, a Martin-Bell power boosted tail gun emplacement, and larger tail surfaces. Range grew to 1,150 miles. Bomb load was decreased to 3,000 pounds.[5]

B-26C

The C-model Marauder was, in effect, a B-model built at Martin's Omaha, Nebraska facility, where production of B-26Cs reached 1,235 aircraft. The big wing and enlarged tail, plus other weighty additions, took

their toll as C-models (and late B-models) posted a top speed around 282 miles an hour and a cruising speed that had dropped to 214 miles an hour. The R-2800-43 engine again prevailed with C-models. B-26Cs and late B-models packed a total of 12 .50-caliber machine guns plus a bomb load rated at 3,000 pounds. Range was still around 1,150 miles.[6]

XB-26D

The sole XB-26D was a converted B-26 using ducts from the engine nacelles to heat the wings for de-icing.

B-26E

Only one Marauder was an E-model, and it was another convert from an earlier version, when a B-26B was stripped and modified with a forward location for

Standard AAF portrait depicted the sixth B-26C (41-34678). Double fore-and-aft scissors on nosewheel strut are visible in this view; old-style .50-caliber tail gun emplacement was used on this aircraft. (AAF via Bowers)

A brace of camouflaged tall-tail B-26Bs bracketed an unarmed natural metal finish B-model in a stateside photo probably taken during 1943 when the national insignia was briefly bordered in red. All three aircraft have the late Bell tail gun emplacement. (Martin)

The B-26A (depicted is the third A-model, 41-7347) weighed about 200 pounds more at gross than earlier Marauders. A-models introduced 24-volt electrical systems instead of the earlier 12-volt systems Martin had been using on the bombers. (William T. Larkins via Peter M. Bowers)

External fuselage stiffeners anticipated punishing loads on the XB-26H Middle River Stump Jumper *Marauder.* (AAF/Glen Edwards collection)

the dorsal turret at the navigator's station. (Some AAF documents said the model letter "E" at one time was to be applied to B-26B-1s modified with increased positive camber to increase wing angle of incidence three degrees for better performance. Ultimately, a 3.5-degree incidence change was introduced on the production line for B-26F and G-models, and the use of the E-model designation for this so-called "twisted wing" was dropped by the AAF by November 1943.) The Martin proposal to move the dorsal turret farther forward on production B-26s was rebuffed by the AAF in the face of perceived dwindling requirements for Marauders.[7]

B-26F

The B-26F initiated a significant, if subtle, change to improve Marauder aerodynamics when

the wing was repositioned with 3.5 degrees more incidence, resulting in better takeoff performance and a more level cruise attitude. This also increased, slightly, propeller ground clearance, which could be a concern on rough fields. The F-model omitted the fixed nose gun of earlier versions. Three hundred B-26Fs were built. The B-26F used a pair of R-2800-43 engines.

B-26G

The last production variant of the Marauder was the B-26G, fitted with the wing of increased incidence, a larger life raft compartment, and more universal AN (Army Navy) equipment in place of some of the AAF-unique items on previous models. As with the F-models, all 893 B-26Gs were built at Baltimore, as Omaha became involved in contract pro-

duction of B-29 Superfortresses. B-26Gs also used the Dash-43 version of the R-2800 engine, rated at 1,920 horsepower for takeoff. So similar were B-26Gs in appearance to F-models that serial numbers are often the only way to ascertain the model identity.

XB-26H

To test tandem fuselage-mounted landing gear envisioned for the next generation of jet bombers including Martin's own B-48 and Boeing's B-47 Stratojet, a TB-26G was modified into the one-off H-model configuration. With two sets of mainwheels in the fuselage and outriggers in the engine nacelles, the testbed was nicknamed the *Middle River Stump Jumper*. Its fuselage bore evidence of external stiffeners to accommodate the stresses of testing the unorthodox landing gear.

[1] Peter M. Bowers and Gordon Swanborough, *United States Military Aircraft Since 1908,* Putnam, London, 1971. [2] *Ibid.* [3] *Ibid.* [4] *Case History of B-26 Airplane Project,* Air Force Materiel Command History Office, 22 February 1945. [5] Peter M. Bowers and Gordon Swanborough, *United States Military Aircraft Since 1908,* Putnam, London, 1971. [6] *Ibid.* [7] *Case History of B-26 Airplane Project,* Air Force Materiel Command History Office, 22 February 1945. [8] *Index of AF Serial Numbers To Aircraft 1958 and Prior, Part 1: Numerical Listing,* Procurement Division, MCPPSR (USAF).

Seldom-seen view of the XB-26H in flight. (SDAM)

The XB-26H was a modified G-model (44-68221) fitted with a test version of the tandem main gear and outrigger wheels that would be used on some first-generation postwar American jet bombers like the B-47 and Martin's own XB-48. Though airbrushed to emphasize burning rubber in a tight turn, the photo is a dramatic vignette of testing that led to postwar bomber development. (Martin via Bowers)

The XB-26H was inspected as a photo was taken on 20 January 1947. (Martin via Bowers)

Ultimate production variant of the Marauder was the B-26G, using the 3.5-degree increased-incidence wing first introduced on the F-model. The photo dramatically shows this change, as the engines sweep upward compared with the fuselage profile. All 893 B-26Gs were built at Martin's Baltimore plant. (Frederick A. Johnsen Collection)

Serial Numbers

B-26 variants were assigned blocks of serial numbers as contracts were awarded. Hence, there are irregular gaps between batches of serials. Though this was a simple result of the way in which serial blocks were parceled out, it may have had the additional benefit of obscuring production totals to a watchful enemy. Marauder serials were:[8]

B-26	40-1361 through 40-1561
B-26A	41-7345 through 41-7483
B-26B	41-17544 through 41-18334; 41-31573 through 41-32072; 42-43260 through 42-43357; 42-43360 through 42-43361; 42-43459; 42-95738 through 42-96228
B-26C	41-34673 through 41-35370; 41-35372; 41-35374 through 41-35515; 41-35517 through 41-35538; 41-35540; 41-35548 through 41-35551; 41-35553 through 41-35560; 42-107497 through 42-107855
B-26F	42-96229 through 42-96528
B-26G	43-34115 through 43-34614; 44-67805 through 44-67944; 44-67970 through 44-68221; 44-68254
TB-26G	44-67945 through 44-67969; 44-68222 through 44-68253
AT-23A	42-43358 through 42-43359; 42-43362 through 42-43458; 42-95629 through 42-95737
AT-23B	41-35371; 41-35373; 41-35516; 41-35539; 41-35541 through 41-35547; 41-35552; 41-35561 through 41-35872; 42-107471 through 42-107496

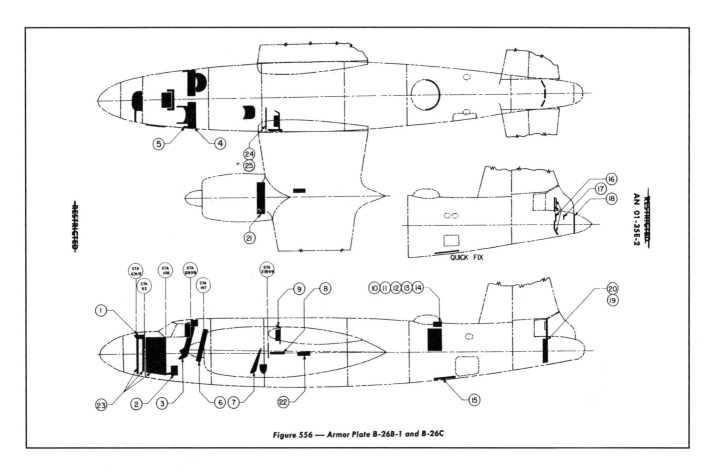

Figure 556 — Armor Plate B-26B-1 and B-26C

Black areas on somewhat stylized early- and late-model B-26 drawings identified placement of armor plate for crew and vital component protection. (Frederick A. Johnsen Collection)

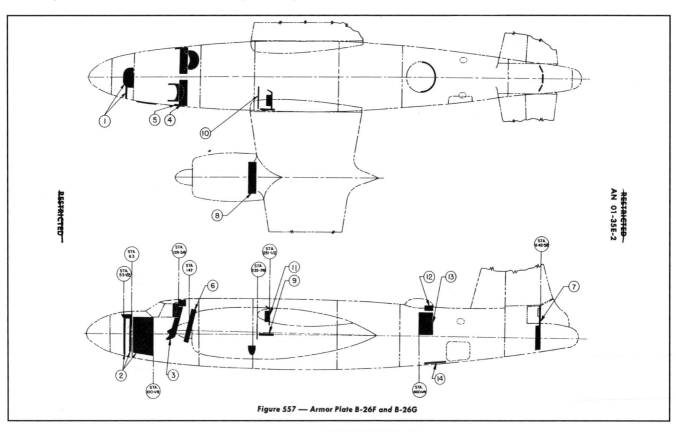

Figure 557 — Armor Plate B-26F and B-26G

B-26 Series

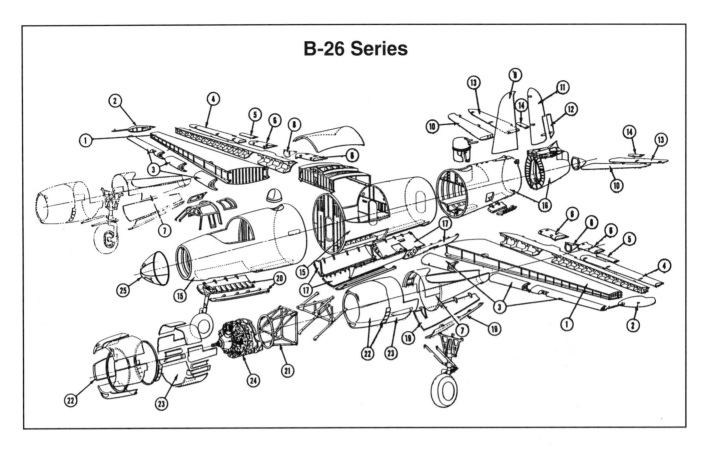

Marauder exploded drawing reveals the pieces that made up the bomber, including a seldom-seen bulbous astrodome that could be placed in the circular dorsal hatch just aft of the cockpit. (Bill Miranda Collection)

Out of the last batch of B-26Bs, Marauder 42-95739 carried the enlarged air scoops above the cowling added during B-model production. (SDAM)

The B-26E, converted from a B-model, had its Martin top turret relocated forward, as photographed in November 1942. (Frederick A. Johnsen Collection)

Forward top turret location on sole B-26E was not adopted for production Marauders; center-of-gravity issues concerned Marauder designers and crews. (Frederick A. Johnsen Collection)

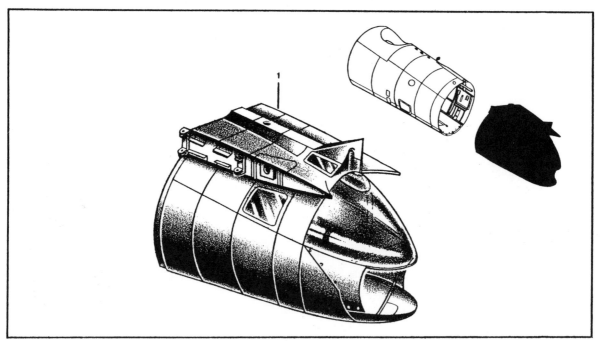

Figure 195 — Aft Section Fuselage

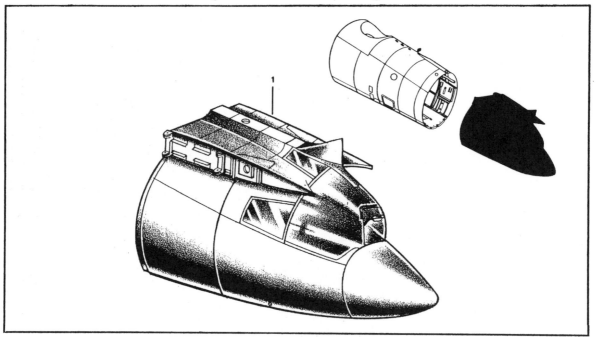

Figure 196 — Aft Section Fuselage

During production of B-26Bs and similar C-models, the tail gun emplacement changed from a pointed metal cap with two hand-held .50-caliber guns protruding above it (Figure 196) to a more blunt tail with more Plexiglas enclosing a hydraulically-boosted pair of .50-calibers (Figure 195). The change to the rounded hydraulically-boosted tail emplacement took place beginning with the introduction of the B-26B-20 and the B-26C-10 production blocks. (Frederick A. Johnsen Collection)

FULL OF **3** FIGHT

The U.S. Army Air Forces sent B-26 Marauders into climates as diverse as the heat of the North African desert, temperate western Europe, the tropics of the Pacific, and the dank chill of Alaska. The European Theater of Operations (ETO) hosted a high of 1,012 Martin B-26s by the end of November 1944. At war's end in Europe, more than 800 B-26s were still counted in the ETO by the AAF.

Marauders came to the Mediterranean Theater of Operations (MTO) in November 1942, starting with 14 aircraft and growing, with a few setbacks, until peaking at 321 Marauders in April 1944. As the war against Germany wound down, by the end of April 1945, only six B-26s were listed in the MTO. In Pacific Ocean Areas, defined by the AAF as including Seventh Air Force before July 1945 and Air Forces in Middle

Pacific (AIRFORMIDPAC) after that time, Marauders only briefly appeared, numbering three aircraft in May and 14 in June 1942. The high point of Marauders arrayed against the Japanese in Alaska was only 29 B-26s, attained in June 1942 during the height of Japanese activity in the Aleutians concurrent with the move against Midway. Under the general heading of *Theaters vs. Japan*, the AAF showed B-26s

Viewed from above, the third B-26A (41-7347) showed medium green blotching applied to the edges of its wings and tail surfaces in an effort to break up long straight lines and render the bomber less visible. (AAF via Bowers)

B-26B-1-MA (41-17863) crumpled one of its Curtiss Electric propellers in a careening mishap at La Senia, Algeria, on 15 June 1943. Pilot's overhead hatch hinged on the outside edge. (Kenneth M. Sumney)

Wearing a yellow band around its fuselage star indicating service in North Africa, B-26B 41-17724 crumpled its nose and buckled the aft fuselage in a June 1943 landing mishap at La Siena. (Kenneth M. Sumney via Peter M. Bowers)

present throughout 1942 and into early 1943, but the numbers were small, topping out at only 43 Marauders logged at the end of June 1942.[1]

Marauders Around the World

When the AAF tumbled into combat after Pearl Harbor, even the best-laid prewar plans of procurement and supply were strained by the realities of not enough aircraft to reach too many targets. The urge to dispatch every available warplane to see action wherever needed had to be tempered by the realities of logistics, which were better served by concentrating some types of aircraft in some theaters. In 1942, B-26 Marauders were dispatched to Alaska, the Pacific, and into the Middle East and Europe. Over the next year, the geographic footprint of the Marauder would see its withdrawal from the Pacific and Alaska, plus a profound realignment of Marauder assets out of Eighth Air Force and into Ninth Air Force for use against the European Continent.

Martin B-26 combat in the AAF included:

1942: By 4 May 1942, Fifth Air Force B-26 Marauders of the 22nd Bomb Group were bombing Vunakanau Airfield on Rabaul. Throughout the month, the pioneering combat Marauders of the 22nd Bomb Group launched sorties against seaplane bases, airfields, and other targets around Lae and Rabaul. An airfield attack against Lae on 24 May 1942 was sobering as heavy flak and about 15 Japanese fighters succeeded in throwing the Marauder crews' bombing accuracy off. Several B-26s were lost or damaged that day.[2]

Japanese efforts to mount attacks simultaneously in the Aleutian Islands and at Midway in June 1942 were met in part by Marauders, as on 3 June when a half-dozen B-26s of the 11th Air Force launched an unsuccessful search for the Japanese carrier force that had completed an attack on Dutch Harbor that day. The next day, four torpedo-wielding B-26s from Seventh Air Force challenged the Japanese fleet at Midway; though the crews pressed attacks bravely, results with

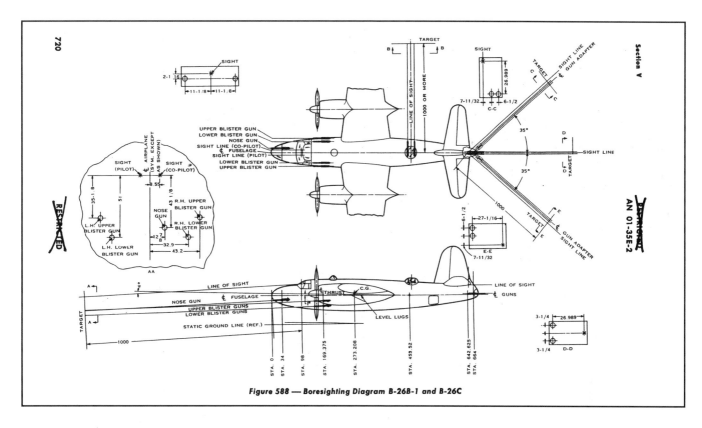

Figure 588 — Boresighting Diagram B-26B-1 and B-26C

Drawings from a Marauder erection and maintenance technical order show gun boresighting measurements for early and late B-26 models. The angled thrust line of F- and G-models is marked. Fixed forward-firing guns were angled downward to facilitate ground attack. Tail guns had a 70-degree lateral field of fire, with 35 degrees either side of center. (Frederick A. Johnsen Collection)

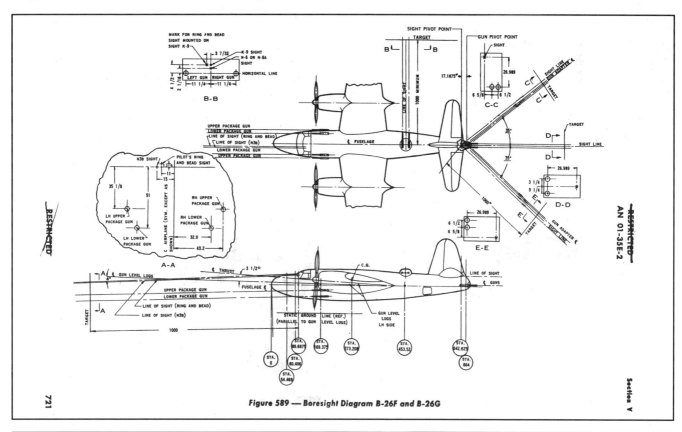

Figure 589 — Boresight Diagram B-26F and B-26G

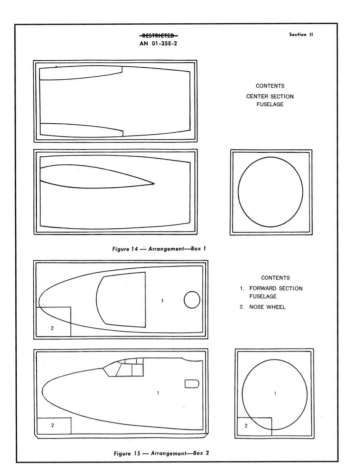

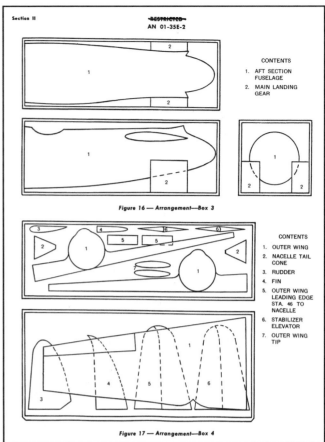

The B-26 could be disassembled and crated for shipment if need be, as sketched for a Marauder erection and maintenance manual. (Frederick A. Johnsen Collection)

Marauders and torpedoes were unsatisfying. That same day, over the Aleutians, five 11th Air Force B-26s joined a pair of B-17s to attack the lurking Japanese carrier force, while a trio of Marauders went after the enemy cruiser *Takao*. Hits were not scored. The inexperience of 1942 would lead to more productive Marauder sorties as the war evolved.[3]

Marauder combat remained the province of a few B-26s arrayed against the Japanese through the summer of 1942, as on 21 July when Marauders from Fifth Air Force attacked a convoy near Salamaua as it steamed toward a landing site at Buna. The Japanese succeeded in forestalling Allied efforts to claim the same

area at this time. B-26s from Fifth Air Force repeatedly attacked the Japanese around Gona as the enemy army pushed on toward Kokoda in the interior of New Guinea. Airfields at Lae and Salamaua, northwest to the Japanese rear, were important targets for the Marauders as the enemy continued to reach toward the Owen Stanley Mountains to the southeast. The limited resources were frustrating as the Marauders and other warplanes of Fifth Air Force repeatedly targeted the advancing Japanese. As Japanese troops continued applying pressure southward to the Owen Stanleys, Marauders and other Allied bombers and fighters also had to contend with a Japanese force to the east, at Milne Bay.

New Guinea was under a desperate siege in 1942, and a few Fifth Air Force B-26 crews contributed what they could to ultimately keep the rugged country from falling under complete control of the Japanese. Hardy Australian troops pressed the enemy back from Milne Bay that September even as other Australian forces were compelled to fall back to defensive positions in the Owen Stanley Range to the northwest.[4]

Meanwhile, in the dank Aleutian area, 11th Air Force B-26s pulled reconnaissance duty in an inhospitable climate. On 14 October 1942, a half-dozen 11th Air Force Marauders contributed to a strike against the Japanese outpost established on Kiska. The next

day, three Aleutian Marauders set fire to a large cargo ship in Gertrude Cove, as well as striking Attu. Japanese antiaircraft fire downed one of the B-26s. On 16 October an 11th Air Force B-26 was shot down in missions involving six Marauders, a B-17, and four P-38s near Kiska. As a result of this attack, two Japanese destroyers were reported sunk.[5]

As Japanese naval forces repeatedly bombarded Henderson Field on Guadalcanal in late 1942, the arrival of even three B-26s at Henderson on 13 November was welcomed by its beleaguered defenders. Two days later, a naval surface fleet turned back the Japanese fleet and sank the battleship *Kirishima,* while losing a destroyer, as the naval battle for Guadalcanal subsided. Even as Pacific B-26s continued to bomb Japanese supplies and transportation in New Guinea and up in the Aleutians late in 1942, a new B-26 theater of operations was inaugurated on 28 November 1942 when the 12th Air Force's 319th Bomb Group, new to North Africa and the Mediterranean, first sent B-26s

to bomb oil, train yards, and warehouses in Sfax.

The 319th was joined by another 12th Air Force Marauder unit, the 17th Bomb Group, which began operations with a six-ship strike over the airdrome at Gabes in the face of flak and Bf-109 fighters on 30 December 1942. Over North Africa, the B-26s sometimes had the benefit of fighter cover from P-38s as the Marauders targeted transportation and supply assets of Axis forces.[6]

As Marauders continued to prosecute the war in diverse parts of the Pacific as well as in the Mediterranean, the last day of 1942 was noted on Guadalcanal by the arrival of B-26s from the 69th Bomb Squadron.

1943: Fifth Air Force's veteran 22nd Bomb Group was understrength at 32 B-26s by January 1943. At that time, the 22nd's Marauders were withdrawn from combat, refurbished, and returned under the auspices of the 22nd's 19th Bomb Squadron, while the other squadrons of the 22nd

Group converted to B-25 Mitchells. The 19th Bomb Squadron flew Marauders in combat around New Guinea until they were finally taken out of service in January 1944.[7]

By April 1943, the only two Marauder squadrons in the 13th Air Force, the 69th and 70th Bomb Squadrons of the 42nd Bomb Group, traded their B-26s for B-25s.[8] The supply of Martin B-26s for combat was being narrowed to European and Mediterranean service during 1943, and Pacific service was in small numbers.

The Fifth, 11th, 12th, and 13th Air Forces all had some Marauders in January 1943. The B-26s of the 12th Air Force continued attacking transportation, airfield, and shipping targets in North Africa. Thirteenth Air Force B-26s participated in the Guadalcanal fighting. Early that month 11th Air Force posted Alaskan B-26 sorties.

The growth in Marauder operations was taking place in the North Africa, and later the Mediterranean and European,

Invasion stripes helped identify this B-26 (possibly B-model 42-95909; maybe of 344th Bomb Group) to friendly troops. The Marauder parked with a Mustang at airfield A-9, LeMolay, France, in August 1944. (Fred LePage Collection)

Flak ravaged the left wing and aft part of the nacelle of B-26B 41-17747, causing a large curl of wing skin to roll out into the slipstream. As the stricken Marauder limped home from a raid over Tunisia, a crewmember used the removable large astrodome atop the forward fuselage to inspect the damage. (AAF via Peter M. Bowers)

Theaters of Operation. Twelfth Air Force's third Marauder bomb group, the 320th, came on scene in April, joining the 17th and 319th Bomb Groups already there. It was here that systematic Marauder operations were honed, as the strength of on-hand B-26s grew, and allowed for more widespread use than in the Pacific.

The other Marauder growth came in England, where the Eighth Air Force received B-26s in February, and first committed them to combat on 14 May 1943. That first Marauder operation by the Eighth Air Force contributed 11 B-26s from the 322nd Bomb Group to a force that also used 198 heavy bombers to strike four targets simultaneously. This total of 209 bombers was the growing Eighth Air Force's first opportunity to

launch more than 200 bombers. The 11 Marauders were assigned to bomb the power station at Ijmuiden in Holland at low level.[9] Roaring in unescorted at 50 feet, bucking to 100 feet altitude to bomb, the Marauders had few telling bomb strikes on the power station that day. On the run home, some of the B-26s flew higher, encountering more flak. One crashed in England, others had shrapnel damage and some wounded aboard. The intensity of antiaircraft fire over Western Europe served a warning that day.

Three days later, the 322nd was sent back to strike Ijmuiden and another power station at Haarlem, again at minimum altitude. One B-26 aborted on the way over the North Sea. The small B-26 force entered the Continent at the

wrong spot, as aggressive antiaircraft fire claimed the mission leader and another Marauder. Others, by then off course, bombed a target in the vicinity of Amsterdam. Of the 10 Marauders reaching the Continent on 17 May 1943, all were lost due to antiaircraft fire, a collision between two of the B-26s, and Bf-109 attacks as the last two survivors scrambled back across the North Sea toward England. The bravery of the Marauder men would not be used this way again; the second Ijmuiden mission prompted a stand-down for the fledgling B-26s of the Eighth Air Force, and a rethinking of using its Marauders on low-level raids.[10]

While Eighth Air Force recovered from its early Marauder massacre, B-26s assigned to North-

west African Air Forces (NAAF) repeatedly hit targets including Pantelleria, on the path to Sicily, as preparations for the aerial and amphibious invasion of Sicily unfolded. Marauders bombed targets in Sicily on 9 July 1943; the night of 9/10 July, the Allied army assault on Sicily was launched.[11]

Eighth Air Force B-26s returned to the fight on 16 July 1943 when 14 Marauders attacked the railyards at Abbeville. This mission marked the beginning of operations by VIII Air Support Command, in charge of the 322nd, 323rd, 386th, and 387th Bomb Groups, all equipped with B-26s. The Eighth Air Force Marauders made other small raids on western European targets including airfields and coke ovens in July. By 4 August, Eighth Air Force posted 33 B-26s on a strike against the shipyards at Le Trait. But the Eighth's use of Marauders was short lived, as a realignment of assets placed all of these B-26 bomb groups in Ninth Air Force as of 16 October 1943.[12]

Marauders of NAAF cast shadows over Naples on 17 July as part of a force of more than 200 B-26s, B-25s, and B-17s that concentrated on marshaling yards. On 21 July, the contingent of Fifth Air Force B-26s bombed Japanese barges and jetties to the west of Voco Point, continuing activities around the Solomon Sea for the remainder of the month. On 13 August 1943, Fifth Air Force B-26s were part of a total force of 59 bombers including B-17s and B-24s that dropped 175 tons of bombs in the vicinity of Salamaua, making this the heaviest one-day strike to date for Fifth Air

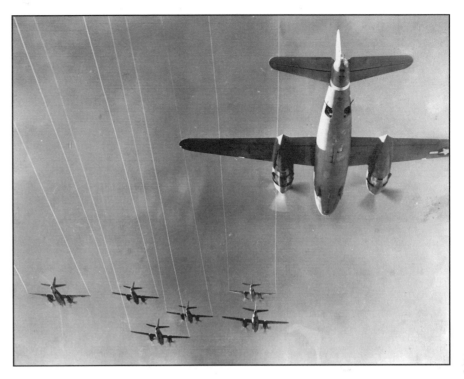

Wingtip condensation streamers etched the sky behind a formation of Marauders over Europe. Low-mounted waist window openings are evident on B-26 closest to camera. (AAF/Martin)

The date on the bottom of the photo, 14 May 43, agrees with the penned caption: "First Marauder Raid". This was the B-26's Eighth Air Force debut, watched with some anticipation. (AAF)

Force. As the summer months of 1943 passed, NAAF B-26s repeatedly were sent to bomb transportation-related targets in Italy, including airfields, marshaling yards, and bridges. Marauders hit Europe from two sides on 22 August as 35 B-26s from Eighth Air Force bombed the airfield at Beaumont-le-Roger as B-26s, escorted by A-36 attack variants of the P-51, struck at the marshaling yards of Salerno. The Salerno strike force of Marauders and A-36s jointly claimed the destruction of 26 Axis fighters.[13]

By 15 September 1943, Eighth Air Force mustered about 70 B-26s for a strike on the German-held airfield at Merville. The next day, over Lae, Fifth Air Force B-26s joined other bombers to hit Japanese positions prior to the occupation of Lae by Australian forces. In September, Fifth Air Force's Marauders would also strike Finschafen in preparation for an Allied amphibious invasion there on 22 September. On 27 September, Eighth Air Force logged more than 130 Marauder sorties against airfields at Conches and Beauvais/Tille. Weather foiled all but six of 72 Eighth Air Force B-26s launched on 2 Octo-

ber 1943 against airfield targets in France, as the majority of the Marauder crews refrained from bombing because cloud cover made target identification impossible. This pointed out a dilemma for Allied bomber crews, as Western Europe was under German occupation. Targets in occupied countries frequently were spared in inclement weather to avoid the possibility of collateral damage occurring to the friendly civilian populace. Even as the era of Eighth Air Force Marauder units drew to a close, the B-26s of the Eighth's four Marauder groups reached ever-higher sor-

In full Normandy Invasion regalia, a B-26B (42-96120) of the 397th Bomb Group's 597th Bomb Squadron was a likely subject for photography. Black-and-white invasion stripes were ordered taken off in stages, with the markings on top of the wings first to be removed by about July 1944. (Merhar/AFHRA)

tie rates, as on 3 October when nearly 200 B-26 sorties were tallied against airfields at four sites on the Continent.[14] The frequent use of Marauders against German-held airfields in western Europe was intended to inhibit the Luftwaffe's ability to use these fighters against ongoing Eighth Air Force heavy bomber formations.[15]

By 28 November 1943, B-26s from Italian bases were ranging over Southern France, although that day the medium bombers were recalled because of bad weather. Over the French coast, the Marauders and their fighter escort were challenged by German fighters, five of whom were claimed as victories. Ninth Air Force sent B-26s for the first time to troublesome V-weapon launch sites on 5 December 1943 only to abandon the mission when cloud cover made the outcome dubious. Two days later over Italy, the difficult winter hindered operations severely, although a lone Marauder managed to attack a bridge south of Arma di Taggia. Operating under the mantle of 15th Air Force, B-26s demolished a highway bridge and damaged a rail bridge on the Var River on 18 December, while other Marauders from 15th Air Force scored near misses on a viaduct at Antheor. In December, the B-26s still in Fifth Air Force were active in continued strikes at Finschafen and pre-invasion operations against New Britain. A 29 December Fifth Air Force mission included B-26s in attacks aimed at Cape Gloucester on New Britain as U.S. Marines moved to take the airfield there from the Japanese. Meanwhile, weather permitting, Ninth Air Force continued to apply Marauders to bombing the V-weapon sites in Western Europe as 1943 drew to a close. On the last day of the year, Ninth Air Force logged about 200 B-26 sorties against V-weapon sites in coastal France.[16]

Exceptions abound to any regulation on aircraft markings, as the relationship of invasion stripes to the upper wing star on this Marauder show, when compared to the photo of B-26B 41-31918 on the opposite page. The insignia is outboard of the stripes, while the wing insignia of 41-31918 impinges on the outboard white stripe. (Merhar/AFHRA)

1944: A realignment of units on 1 January 1944 transferred three B-26 groups from the jurisdiction of 15th Air Force to 12th Air Force. The next day, some of these 12th Air Force Marauders bombed bridges at Riva Santo Stefano and Ventimiglia, as well as targeting a bridge over the Var River and railyards at Arma di Taggia. The hard-working Marauders in Fifth Air Force, along with B-25s, logged a strike against Madang on the Bismark Sea coast of New Guinea on 2 January 1944. Two days later, Ninth Air Force mounted 253 Marauder sorties against NOBALL sites (as V-weapon targets were coded). Twelfth Air Force B-26s logged an unusual nocturnal mission the night of 10/11 January 1944 when they hit the iron and steel works at Piombino. It was a period of return engagements over NOBALL sites

in France and transportation and construction targets in Italy for Marauders, as the drawn-out aerial siege of Europe demanded persistence in the face of enemy reconstruction, and sometimes-crippling weather.[17]

Sometimes, as on 15 February 1944, Ninth Air Force launched a morning and an afternoon Marauder strike, targeting V-weapons sites in France as well as airfields. That same day, 12th Air Force B-26s joined B-25s in bombing the contested Monte Cassino Benedictine Abbey. Though not often considered a battlefield tactical weapon, Marauders from 12th Air Force struck at troop concentrations along roads around Vallalta on 20 February. On 21 February, Ninth Air Force inaugurated Pathfinder blind bombing opera-

tions during a B-26 raid on Coxyde airfield — 18 Marauders bombed while nearly 190 aborted due to weather.[18]

Ninth Air Force sent 22 Marauders to bomb German-held airfields at Deelen, Leeuwarden, and Gilze-Rijen on the morning of 24 February 1944, to disrupt Luftwaffe fighter activity in advance of American heavy bomber overflights of the Continent that day. That afternoon, 145 Marauders were counted by Ninth Air Force in strikes against NOBALL targets between Abbeville and Saint-Omer. The next morning, 191 Ninth Air Force B-26s bombed airfields in France again as a diversion to aid Eighth Air Force heavy bombers dispatched over four major strategic targets in Germany. The routine for Ninth Air Force Marauders during this

In the summer of 1944, invasion stripes wrapped around the fuselage of this 455th Bomb Squadron, 323rd Bomb Group, B-26C (42-107692). (Fred LePage Collection)

Camouflaged B-model (41-31918) carried the white tail band of the 323rd Bomb Group; fuselage letters "RJ" denoted the 454th Bomb Squadron. (AAF)

time period primarily revolved around airfield, marshaling yard, and NOBALL strikes.[19]

The storied city of Rome reverberated under the beat of R-2800 engines turning four-blade propellers as B-26s from 12th Air Force attacked the Rome and Tiburtina marshaling yards on 8 and 10 March. The fighting in Italy included major efforts to deny German forces the transportation they needed to keep supplied. Back over Holland, Ninth Air Force returned to bloody Ijmuiden on 26 March with a powerful force of 338 B-26s and 35 Douglas A-20s to attack German torpedo-boat facilities. The next day, Ninth Air Force B-26s went after V-weapon sites in Northern France; some of

these Marauders had to abort because of problems with blind-bombing equipment. Inclement weather closed down Ninth Air Force medium bomber activity until 8 April. On 29 March 1944, over Elba, B-26s manned by French aircrews attached to 12th Air Force dropped bombs on Portoferraio.[20]

As the spring of 1944 aged on the calendar, Ninth Air Force B-26 target lists came to include German coastal guns and other military installations on the French coast, in preparation for the planned summer invasion of the Continent. All types of AAF warplanes participated in coastal strikes, some of which were deliberate deceptions, striking regions other than Normandy in

an effort to keep the Germans guessing where the invasion would take place.

On 18 April 1944, 277 B-26s from Ninth Air Force and 37 A-20s bombed gun positions and marshaling yards at Dunkirk, Calais, and Charleroi/Saint Martin. Two dozen of the Marauders dropped Window — foil chaff to cloud German radar scopes. On the following day, even as their Marauders bombed targets on the Continent, elements of Ninth Air Force in England began a training exercise in preparation of the planned eventual movement of Ninth Air Force units to Continental Europe once ground forces secured appropriate airfields. Four B-26s from Ninth Air Force succumbed during a 236-

The beauty of a bare metal Marauder like this one could quickly turn ugly if its reflective surface made it more visible to the Germans. A number of silver B-26s were oversprayed later when they moved onto the Continent to minimize their detection from above. (AFHRA)

Marauder effort against a variety of V-weapon, coastal defense, and gun positions on 21 April. During this stage in the war, 12th Air Force Marauders continued the war against German transportation capacity in Italy, often bombing bridges. Weather was not always cooperative, and some days all Marauder operations of both Ninth and 12th Air Forces were canceled.[21] The zenith of Mediterranean AAF B-26 operations was achieved in April 1944 when 321 Marauders were tallied in the Mediterranean Theater of Operations.[22]

Ninth Air Force became the major user of Marauders. Its eighth and final B-26 bomb group, the 397th, became operational on 20 April 1944.[23] Ninth Air Force used this capacity to inaugurate its participation in the pre-invasion offensive against German airfields on 11 May 1944 by sending more than 330 B-26s over Luftwaffe bases at Beaumont-le-Roger and Cormeilles-en-Vexin, as well as marshaling yards at Mezieres/Charleville and Aerschot.[24]

As Allied ground forces successfully challenged the Gustav Line in Italy, on 17 May 1944 12th Air Force Marauders bombed road bridges in the battlefield area in an effort to isolate German forces. Fifteen B-26s from Ninth Air Force made a pre-dawn raid on the airfield at Beaumont-le-Roger on 23 May; that afternoon 58 Marauders from Ninth Air Force hit a variety of coastal batteries. The availability of B-26s allowed AAF planners to use them on missions within their range, thereby saving heavy four-engine B-17s and B-24s for more distant targets.[25]

The invasion of Europe on 6 June 1944 saw Ninth Air Force log more than 800 B-26 and A-20 sorties that day against coastal gun batteries, road and rail junctions and bridges, and marshaling yards in an effort to dilute German firepower and hobble enemy transportation to the battlefield. This pattern con-

tinued several days into the invasion, as on 8 June when about 400 B-26 sorties targeted transportation as well as enemy fuel storage, ammunition dumps, and troop concentrations in the vicinity of Calais. As the ground fighting in western France evolved, Ninth Air Force Marauders and A-20s interdicted rail lines south-west of Paris and highways south of the Normandy beachhead on 14 June. While V-1s began blindly reaching out to southern England in June, about 370 Ninth Air Force B-26s and A-20s were tasked to bomb a total of nine V-weapon sites in France as well as a coastal defense battery at Houlgate on 20 June 1944. The next day, the Ninth sent Marauders and A-20s against 13 V-weapon sites in the Pas de Calais vicinity.[26]

On 22 June as the Allied ground assault inland progressed, Ninth Air Force B-26s and A-20s hit a series of strongpoints chosen by the U.S. First Army. The bombers delivered an aerial barrage for nearly an hour, moving northward in advance of ground troops. The last day of June saw about 125 B-26s and A-20s from Ninth Air Force use blind-bombing techniques against fuel dumps and road junctions in France when bad weather made visual tech-

The first batch of Marauders over Western Europe on 14 May 1943 included Chickasaw Chief, *a B-26B (41-17999).* (AAF)

The 322nd Bomb Group put 11 B-26s aloft for the first Eighth Air Force Marauder attack on 14 May 1943. (AAF)

A Cletrac towed a sled bearing crewmen toward a Marauder of the 391st Bomb Group in France during January 1945. Snow added another element to maintenance of aircraft outdoors on French airfields. (AAF)

niques unworkable. The use of blind bombing over occupied France by medium bombers was in contrast to the methods generally employed by Eighth Air Force heavy bombers, who tended to reserve blind bombing for targets on German soil.

Again on the Fourth of July 1944, 95 Ninth Air Force Marauders and A-20s took advantage of Pathfinder aircraft as they bombed a train bridge at Oissel and stoutly defended German positions north of Anneville-sur-Mer. When weather again hampered Ninth Air Force operations on 14 July, 62 B-26s and A-20s relied on OBOE (a British radar device

using two ground stations to lead an aircraft to a predetermined point) to bomb a railroad embankment at Bourth and a train bridge at Merey. And in Italy, Marauders of the 12th Air Force continued to target bridges and other transportation infrastructure during this part of the summer. Europe's weather played havoc with AAF operations on 21 July 1944. All Marauder operations in both Ninth and 12th Air Forces were off for that day. Weather groundings and aborts plagued the medium bombers often during the year, while high-flying radar-directed B-17 and B-24 heavy bombers continued to hit targets in Germany.[27]

As fighting in Western France continued, Ninth Air Force Marauders and A-20s came to the aid of the U.S. First Army repeatedly. On 30 July, the B-26s and A-20s of Ninth Air Force bombed German defenses in the vicinity of Chaumont. By 2 August, IX Bomber Command of Ninth Air Force removed from its target lists bridges, fuel dumps, and similar targets in Brittany unless specifically requested by the 12th Army Group. This action was for the benefit of the advancing Third Army, which wanted to use the bridges and have access to abandoned stores of German fuel as the logistics of supplying the

Allies on the Continent could not always keep sufficient petroleum flowing at this stage of the war.[28]

By August, Ninth Air Force B-26s were participating in rail interdiction sorties covering a wide area around Paris in an effort to inhibit German military movements. On 11 August 1944, out of 12th Air Force, Marauders joined with B-25s and P-47s to target German gun emplacements along the French and Italian Mediterranean coastlines west of Genoa. These attacks were coordinated in an effort to neutralize the guns as the Allied invasion force for Southern France moved out from Naples under the operation code name Dragoon. As 12th Air Force Marauders continued their support of Dragoon, during the night of 13/14 August, Ninth Air Force sent 28 B-26s on a nocturnal raid over a German ammunition dump and bivouac in the vicinity of Foret de Halouze. Ninth's Marauders continued to hit German rear areas in France, targeting road and rail targets to inhibit the retreat of German troops. On 15 August, 12th Air Force B-26s along with other aircraft hit coastal targets in Southern France as Allied armies landed at several locations there. Later in the day as friendly troops were ashore, the 12th Air Force's bombardment effort moved inland to interdict enemy transportation by targeting vital bridges. The Dragoon troops would not be repulsed, and Marauders played a role in guaranteeing that outcome. By 19 August 1944, 12th Air Force B-26s and B-25s were on the rampage throughout Southeastern France, attacking road and train bridges to slow German movements. The next day these Mediterranean B-26s, along with fighter-bombers and fighters, hit coastal defense guns in the Toulon vicinity.[29]

Even as the invasion of Southern France required medium bomber support in August 1944, targets in Italy's Po River Valley could not be ignored. On 22 August as weather inhibited strikes in Southern France, 12th Air Force Marauders destroyed one Po bridge and wrought serious damage to another.

By 25 August 1944, Paris was liberated. Still, fighting in western Europe would require Ninth Air Force B-26 sorties well into 1945.

A brace of B-26s from the 449th Bomb Squadron, 322nd Bomb Group, cruised above an undercast, with a B-model leading a B-26C. Carrying the star insignia with no white bars helps date the photo somewhere between May and probably July 1943. (AAF)

Twelfth Air Force's use of B-26s as bridge-busters was augmented on 28 August when B-26s attacked the Villafranca di Verona Airfield, destroying several aircraft at the field. The Marauders also did damage to a bridge at Parma. On 9 September 1944, it was back to the bridges for 12th Air Force B-26s, which chalked up good successes against train bridge spans in the eastern part of the Po Valley. On 11 September, the Marauders of 12th Air Force targeted German army positions to assist the U.S. Fifth Army in its push through north-ern Italian mountain passes on the way toward the Gothic Line defenses. The next day, these Marauders attacked German positions in the central battle area of the Gothic Line. Mediterranean Marauders would continue pressure on the Po Valley transportation infrastructure into the autumn of 1944. On 15 October 1944, 12th Air Force B-26s bombed bridges in the east part of the Po Valley and achieved a spectacular success by scoring telling hits on an earthen railroad fill at Ossenigo, trapping more than 300 train cars north of the bombed rail line. Ninth Air Force Marauder targets in the fall of 1944 included fuel and ammunition stores, as well as targets around Brest, which the Allies wanted to capture for its port. Occasionally, Ninth Air Force B-26s flew leaflet missions over parts of France and Belgium.[30]

On 7 October 1944, Ninth Air Force canceled its previous embargo against bombing bridges, opening all bridges on the U.S. front to attacks except those over the Rhine River. When Pathfinder equipment malfunctioned on 11 October, a group of Ninth Air Force Marauders and A-20s had to abort a planned mission to hit the military camp at Camp-de-Bitche because bad weather made visual bombing impossible. The attack was rescheduled the following day. Bridge strikes continued to be the order of the day for many 12th Air Force Marauders. On 4 November more than 200 B-26s and B-25s hit train and road bridges in the Brenner Pass. Brenner and the Po Valley constituted the Germans' two principal routes of supply from the north.[31] By 19 November 1944, Ninth Air Force was logging mission totals that included both B-26 Marauders and new Douglas A-26 Invaders. Not apparent at that early date was the reign of confusion that would ensue several years later when all B-26 Marauders were retired by the Air Force and the surviving A-26 Invaders were redesignated B-26s as part of a sweeping nomenclature change in the service. By the late fall of 1944, Ninth Air Force Marauders were ranging into Germany proper as they carried out missions of interdiction and support for ground operations.

Gremlin, *a B-26B (41-18029) destined for the 387th Bomb Group in England, was delayed in getting to England in 1943 when pilot Lt. Stuart H. Perrin contracted malaria during the delivery flight overseas. By the time* Gremlin *arrived in England, newer Marauders may have superceded it in the Group, and it is believed* Gremlin *never flew combat. Evidence of taped openings on package gun fairings suggests the photos were taken as* Gremlin *was made ready for its overseas journey.* (Stuart H. Perrin family via Cam Martin)

WARBIRDTECH
S E R I E S

A grim reminder that the German war machine still had some fight remaining came two days before Christmas 1944 when Ninth Air Force lost more than 30 bombers out of a combined force of nearly 500 B-26s and A-20s sent to attack transportation targets, villages, and targets of opportunity in Germany. The overwhelming majority of the Ninth's bombers destroyed that day were Marauders.[32]

1945: As early as November 1944, Mediterranean Marauder strength in the AAF dwindled from only 93 B-26s down to 22 the following month. This was reduced to a scant 14 AAF B-26s listed in the MTO in January 1945. (Much of this can be traced to the veteran 319th Bomb Group's transition into B-25s from its B-26s.) By contrast, in the European Theater of Operations where Ninth Air Force had perfected its use of the Marauder, 952 Martin B-26s were counted in the AAF inventory for January 1945.[33]

Ninth Air Force B-26s continued hitting train bridges and road targets in January, weather permitting. They ranged over Western Europe into Germany, sometimes striking at German troop concentrations, and other times targeting infrastructure like bridges in an effort to hinder the movement of those troops. The use of Marauders to help shape the ground battle was illustrated on 2 February 1945 when a mixed total of about 350 B-26, A-20, and A-26 sorties were logged by Ninth Air Force in an effort to bomb road and rail bridges to block the east-west movement of Germans east of the Rhine River, as well as defended spots east of the battle line in Western Germany.[34]

The war was almost over when these Marauder crewmen of the 323rd Bomb Group grabbed quick sandwiches and coffee before flying their second mission of the day, circa April 1945. As captured by an Army Air Forces photographer, the tableau showed variety in B-26 aircrew apparel as the men gathered behind a truck parked on pierced steel planking (PSP) runway matting. (Ninth AF)

Flak ripped open the waist section of this 391st Bomb Group Marauder circa December 1944 as the medium bombers took the war ever deeper on the Continent. (AAF)

cert with the U.S. Ninth and British Second Armies as they crossed the Rhine in Operations Plunder (land-based) and Varsity (airborne). Sometimes, oil storage and ordnance facilities were Ninth Air Force targets in this time too. On 14 April, 18 B-26s from Ninth Air Force dropped leaflets in the Ruhr area.[35]

Marauders met Me-262 jet fighters in the closing days of the war, and on 9 April 1945, a B-26 gunner in the 387th Bomb Group shot down one of the swift German jets. Probably the last AAF Marauder combat came on 3 May 1945 (also the date of Ninth Air Force's final combat mission of the war) when eight special Pathfinder-equipped B-26s from the First Pathfinder Squadron (Provisional) led about 130 A-26 Invaders over German targets.[36]

By 18 February 1945, 60-plus escorted Marauders from Ninth Air Force hit a variety of targets in Germany intended to isolate the Ruhr. AAF Marauders in the European Theater of Operations returned to low-level combat for the first time since 1943 on 22 February 1945 as part of Operation Clarion, a joint AAF/RAF campaign to ruin the already damaged German railway network. The work of disrupting German transportation continued to occupy Ninth Air Force's Marauders well into March. This was emphasized with the 24 March 1945 operations by B-26s, A-26s, and A-20s against transportation and flak targets, in con- The return of peace immediately relaxed the need for so many bombers of all types, and the combat lives of the B-26, B-25, and A-20 quickly were eclipsed in the postwar Air Force by the newer Douglas A-26 Invader, realizing a conversion process that had been hoped for years earlier by some in the AAF.

[1] *Army Air Forces Statistical Digest—World War II,* AAF Office of Statistical Control, December 1945. [2] Kit C. Carter and Robert Mueller, compilers, *Combat Chronology, 1941–1945, U.S. Army Air Forces in World War II,* Center for Air Force History, Washington, D.C., 1991. [3] *Ibid.* [4] *Ibid.* [5] *Ibid.* [6] Kenn C. Rust, *Twelfth Air Force Story,* Historical Aviation Album, Temple City, California, 1975. [7] Steve Birdsall, *Flying Buccaneers—The Illustrated Story of Kenney's Fifth Air Force,* Doubleday, Garden City, New York, 1977. [8] Kenn C. Rust and Dana Bell, *Thirteenth Air Force Story,* Historical Aviation Album, Temple City, California, 1981. [9] Kit C. Carter and Robert Mueller, compilers, *Combat Chronology, 1941–1945, U.S. Army Air Forces in World War II,* Center for Air Force History, Washington, D.C., 1991. [10] Kenn C. Rust, *Eighth Air Force Story,* Historical Aviation Album, Temple City, California, 1978. [11] Kit C. Carter and Robert Mueller, compilers, *Combat Chronology, 1941–1945, U.S. Army Air Forces in World War II,* Center for Air Force History, Washington, D.C., 1991. [12] *Ibid.* [13] *Ibid.* [14] *Ibid.* [15] Roger A. Freeman, *The Mighty Eighth—A History of the U.S. 8th Army Air Force,* Doubleday, Garden City, New York, 1970. [16] Kit C. Carter and Robert Mueller, compilers, *Combat Chronology, 1941–1945, U.S. Army Air Forces in World War II,* Center for Air Force History, Washington, D.C., 1991. [17] *Ibid.* [18] *Ibid.* [19] *Ibid.* [20] *Ibid.* [21] *Ibid.* [22] *Army Air Forces Statistical Digest—World War II,* AAF Office of Statistical Control, December 1945. [23] Kenn C. Rust, *Ninth Air Force Story,* Historical Aviation Album, Temple City, California, 1982. [24] Kit C. Carter and Robert Mueller, compilers, *Combat Chronology, 1941–1945, U.S. Army Air Forces in World War II,* Center for Air Force History, Washington, D.C., 1991. [25] *Ibid.* [26] *Ibid.* [27] *Ibid.* [28] *Ibid.* [29] *Ibid.* [30] *Ibid.* [31] *Ibid.* [32] Kenn C. Rust, *Ninth Air Force Story,* Historical Aviation Album, Temple City, California, 1982; and Kit C. Carter and Robert Mueller, compilers, *Combat Chronology, 1941–1945, U.S. Army Air Forces in World War II,* Center for Air Force History, Washington, D.C., 1991. [33] *Army Air Forces Statistical Digest—World War II,* AAF Office of Statistical Control, December 1945. [34] Kit C. Carter and Robert Mueller, compilers, *Combat Chronology, 1941–1945, U.S. Army Air Forces in World War II,* Center for Air Force History, Washington, D.C., 1991. [35] *Ibid.* [36] Kenn C. Rust, *Ninth Air Force Story,* Historical Aviation Album, Temple City, California, 1982.

MARAUDER 4 MOMENTS

Reports on Marauders in service reveal much about the speedy bomber. Its use in the Battle of Midway helped end its ill-starred excursion as a torpedo bomber.

Launching Torpedoes During the Battle of Midway

The significance of the pending confrontation at Midway Island was not lost on the Americans who gathered what bombers they could there in early June 1942. Loss of the island would deepen the imbalance of power as Japan expanded its sphere of influence; a decisive American victory would not only keep the stars and stripes flying above Midway, but could remove from the watery battlefield key elements of Japan's offensive naval power. Against a lucrative array of Japanese carriers protected by a wilderness of screening warships, four B-26B Marauders each carried one torpedo during a desperate mission on 4 June 1942.

James P. Muri, a first lieutenant who piloted B-26 serial number 42-1391 that day, waited with his crew by their Marauder at 3:15 that morning. At 6 A.M. they warmed up the engines and launched from Midway 25 minutes later. They followed an assigned heading toward the Japanese fleet for an hour and 10 minutes when a concerted attack by fighters and flak hit the small group of four Marauders. Lieutenant Muri managed to penetrate a curtain of flak and fighter fire to release his torpedo at 195 miles an hour from 150 feet above the surface of the waves, sending it toward an aircraft carrier which he then overflew. Now

Evidently photographed while markings were being re-applied, an English-based B-26B (41-31669) carried only a dark disc where fuselage star should be. (AFHRA)

the Marauder's power and streamlining paid off. Lieutenant Muri later reported to VII Bomber Command: "My speed away from the fleet changed considerably, but I was maintaining an indicated air speed of 320 miles per hour. My power setting was full."[1] Lieutenant Muri said his engine instruments showed 2600 rpm and 70 inches of manifold pressure. He estimated the Japanese fighters attacking him as he egressed the area were making 310 miles an hour, enabling his roaring Marauder to outdistance them by an agonizing 10 miles an hour. In the seething cauldron of fire, flak and fighters took their toll, killing the top turret and tail gunners in Lieutenant Muri's Marauder. Yet he managed to bring the damaged bomber back to Midway.[2]

Just ahead of Lieutenant Muri, only Capt. James F. Collins' B-26 remained of the flight of four Marauders. Approaching the Japanese fleet in a diamond formation, the two Marauders to the left and right of center were blown from the sky. Six Navy torpedo bombers arrived at about the same time, possibly to the mutual benefit of both small American formations as Japanese gunners had to decide what to target. Still, a large number of Japanese guns threw out a withering barrage that seemed impenetrable. Captain Collins said he encountered six Japanese fighters, guns blazing, in a head-on attack at about 700 feet until he dived for the water, causing most of their gunfire to zip above the Marauder. In the heat of battle, Captain Collins could not be sure, but he said he thought this was the moment when his two

German officials inspected captured Allied aircraft at a wartime show where this ex-319th Bomb Group Marauder, overpainted in German insignia, was displayed. This B-26B (41-17790) never got the chance to see combat, being lured to a Dutch island by spurious German radio signals after losing one engine on its delivery flight in October 1942. It was test-flown and evaluated by the Luftwaffe during 1943. (Peter M. Bowers Collection)

wingmen, Lieutenants Watson and Mays, were shot down with their crews.[3]

Captain Collins' B-26B released its torpedo about 800 yards from an aircraft carrier; the navigator in the other surviving Marauder said Collins' torpedo entered the water cleanly and was last seen burrowing on a true run toward the Japanese carrier. Early reports vouched that at least two of the Marauders, flown by Captain Collins and the ill-fated Lieutenant Watson, scored hits on aircraft carriers with their single torpedoes;[4] subsequent analysis does not support this. Regardless of hits or misses, the valor of the Marauder men at Midway matched the best efforts of their Navy and Marine counterparts as the B-26s flew into a hail of gunfire so dense the fliers reportedly said they could see projectiles in the air.

Captain Collins and Lieutenant Muri were succinct in their analysis of the B-26B's shortcomings after their run through a gauntlet of death. Collins wrote: "Both turret guns hung up repeatedly. One tail gun would not fire after the first burst. The motors would not pull ammo through the tracks to either tail gun. It had to be jerked back by hand. I consider all guns to have been unsatisfactory during the entire fight. I believe that .50 cal. guns should be out the side windows instead of the .30 guns provided and that 100 round ammo cans should be provided for them instead of the 30 round cans. I believe that at least four .50 cal. guns should be provided fixed in the wings and that a single or twin .50 should be mounted movable in the nose."[5] Captain

In the spring of 1944, the crew of this 323rd Bomb Group B-26 had ample reason to be thankful for flak gear, and for the robust construction of the Marauder, which survived German hits. (AAF)

Collins' remarks presaged ever-increasing arming of subsequent Marauders, including the use of .50-caliber guns in place of the few .30s in early models. Lieutenant Muri echoed the sentiments: "The airplane does not have enough fire power from the front. Several fixed guns are necessary. I had several opportunities to destroy fighter planes with fixed guns. They are also required on the approach to the target. Another vital necessity is support from fighter planes as well as dive bombers."[6]

The Battle of Midway was a stark episode in the evolution of Marauder combat equipment and tactics. Other low-level attacks would follow, but the B-26's war would later be fought from a higher perch.

Up From Africa

In October 1943, 12th Air Force commander Lt. Gen. Carl Spaatz sent General Arnold a publication detailing middle eastern combat experience with a variety of aircraft including the B-26 Marauder, in an effort to better educate new combat units and crews to follow. Interviews with 123 airmen formed the basis for the publication, and included observations like these from Lt. Col. Gordon H. Austin, commander of the 319th Bomb Group: "I think it's the opinion of all pilots who fly the B-26 that it's a good airplane. They're sold on it as the best medium bomber for combat. The B-26 got a reputation for being a 'hot plane' — there were many early losses due to pilots' inexperience. Now the pilots have all the

confidence in the world ... ." This interviewee went on to emphasize: "The B-26 <u>must</u> have close fighter cover."[7]

The 319th Bomb Group operations officer, Maj. Joseph R. Holzapple, was quoted as saying: "We were trained on small formations in low altitude bombing, and now we're using 18 to 36 ships at 8,000 to 12,000 feet — an entire reversal of what we were trained for. ... In the States we bombed from 500 to 2,000 feet using the D-8 bomb sight. We did this for [a] month or so in Africa until losses from light flak made it impracticable; so we went up to 8,000 feet to 12,000 feet using the Norden Sight."

Major Holzapple said that when the B-26 men arrived in the mid-

Bearing RAF markings and serial number FB436, this B-26C-equivalent was operated by the British as a Marauder II. (Bowers Collection)

dle east, "we expected to be a wild, dashing bunch of low-bombing and attacking daredevils." But following some low-level sorties, including mast-top strikes against German shipping in the Mediterranean, enemy fire and fighters were too contentious. The major urged: "Tell the boys at home to practice medium altitude bombing and good formation."[8]

Another 319th Bomb Group pilot was quoted in the report: "I'm just as glad to get away from that low altitude bombing. I was once co-pilot on a sea sweep. We hit a convoy and lost one ship. We got hit and hard, lost one engine but got up to 8,000 feet and five miles from base ran out of gas. We landed her and had a flat tire. That was just too much."[9]

Major Holzapple praised the Marauder for toughness. "They get back all shot to hell; but they're not too good on one engine," he said. He described a common Axis fighter attack: "We are usually attacked from behind and below. Our best defense is to keep that formation tight. Get out of formation and you're a goner; it's essential for our escort to pick up our cripples. … Basically it's a damn good ship. Crews gradually get confidence in it. Those who don't like it are those who don't know it. Personally, I'm damn glad I'm flying in a B-26."[10]

The 319th's armament officer, Capt. Herbert Hartman, reported: "One main worry is to develop a way of taking care of expended cases and links — these fly out and bother the plane behind causing loss of turret domes, windows, leading edges, etc." He also suggested: "If we're through with the rear bomb bay, they should make the release handle with just one slot — eliminate the rear bomb bay slot — which will mean only one operation for the bombardier."[11]

An engineering officer with the 319th Bomb Group lamented the fact that updated tech orders did not always accompany the arrival of improved Marauders. He added: "Tech Orders themselves are now much more interesting — a little hooey and cartoons make them a lot more readable." The lack of spare parts in the MTO in 1943 prompted ingenuity, as the engineering officer reported: "Our mechanics have to do lots of work out of the boneyard.

The first Marauder Mk. III, number HD402, was a B-26F version. Marauder IIIs served with the Royal Air Force and the South African Air Force. (Bowers Collection)

An echelon of three B-26s shows evidence of torpedo shackles installed outside the bomb bay doors. (Merhar/AFHRA)

The other day a ship came in, obviously badly shot up; and [an] enterprising crew chief called in before the ship had landed and asked for a spare tire. He got it."[12]

Maj. Donald Gilbert, 438th Bomb Squadron commander, was quoted as saying: "The B-26 — I used to be a B-25 pilot — had me scared at first. I now consider it the best damn medium made. I like the load it'll carry, its defensive fire power and its maneuverability. New improvements are steadily making it a better plane. It can take a good beating, and lately we've been able to bring her back on one engine. ..." The speed with which American units were sent overseas sometimes resulted in lags in supplies and spare parts deliveries. Major Gilbert had an observation regarding training mechanics in the United States before overseas deployment: "As for our individ-

ual maintenance boys, they're swell at improvising. They've done wonders in making tools, etc. It'd be a good thing for mechanics back home to practice without the proper equipment, develop their inventiveness and ingenuity."[13]

The bad publicity about Marauders had some pilots in the 319th spooked at first, and this could have a detrimental effect on others in the group, including the maintainers of the B-26s. A crew chief observed: "I like the B-26, like it better every day, although I didn't like it when I first started. At first the pilots were scared of it, but as soon as we saw that they got over that and got confidence in the ship and confidence in the men who work on it, we felt the same way. The pilots have now proved they are masters of the plane." Another 319th Bomb Group mechanic criticized the

big-wing Marauder variants: "Only thing I don't like is too much extra wing — slows her down too much."[14]

The litany of experiences in north Africa in the 319th Bomb Group indicated a need for more thorough training in the U.S., and showed a definite learning curve with the hot Marauder that ultimately made believers out of its crews and maintainers.

Establishing a Reputation in England

Marauders flying out of England weathered heavy losses on early missions that once again cast some doubts about the B-26s' ability to perform. But even as they strove to earn a place in the European Theater of Operations, the B-26 crews, according to one newspaper correspondent, showed their pride in

Marauders by dreaming up disparaging nicknames for other AAF warplanes. In the bleak battle season of 1943 when the Eighth Air Force lost many B-17s, the B-26 crews darkly called Fortresses the "Vanishing American," according to a newspaper feature of the time. About the best they could do was call the big, rugged P-47 Thunderbolt fighter "half a B-26."[15]

But the Marauder men of the Eighth Air Force suffered a setback on 17 May 1943 when 10 of 11 B-26s sent on a low-level attack over Holland were downed by fighters and flak. The sole survivor had aborted due to mechanical problems. Out of experiences like this, an ETO rationale for the Marauder saw the B-26 used increasingly at medium altitudes of at least 10,000 feet, with fighter escort, and targeting items of strategic interest.[16]

The subsequent allocation of ETO B-26s to Ninth Air Force coincided with the evolution of medium-altitude tactics that benefited the fast Martins, and secured for them a niche in the great air battles over Western Europe.

Marauders for Britain and the Commonwealth

As early as December 1941, three B-26As were flown to England for evaluation by the Royal Air Force, under the British designation Marauder I. The RAF deemed the Marauder appropriately equipped for warfare in North Africa, and No. 14 Squadron was the first British unit to equip with the type in July of 1942. Four more RAF squadrons subsequently flew Marauders, the first of these beginning in early 1943. Fifty-two Marauder I models used RAF serial numbers FK109 through FK160.[17]

The Royal Air Force sometimes did not see model changes the same way as did the AAF. In British use, 19 B-26Bs were called Marauder IA and given the serials FK362 through FK380. A hundred B-26Cs became the Marauder II (serial numbers FB418 through FB517) in British and South African Air Force use. Two-

Some French Marauders carried national roundels with horizontal bars where U.S. insignia would be, evidently from reassigning American assets to the French. In the photo, taken in August 1944, French Colonel Bouvard, commanding officer of the 34th Bombardment Escadre, presented a Nazi flag to General Webster as a war trophy liberated from Fort Gardane, Toulon, France. The wartime AAF caption for the photo said: "Colonel Bouvard forced the surrender of this German strong point after being taken prisoner." (AAF)

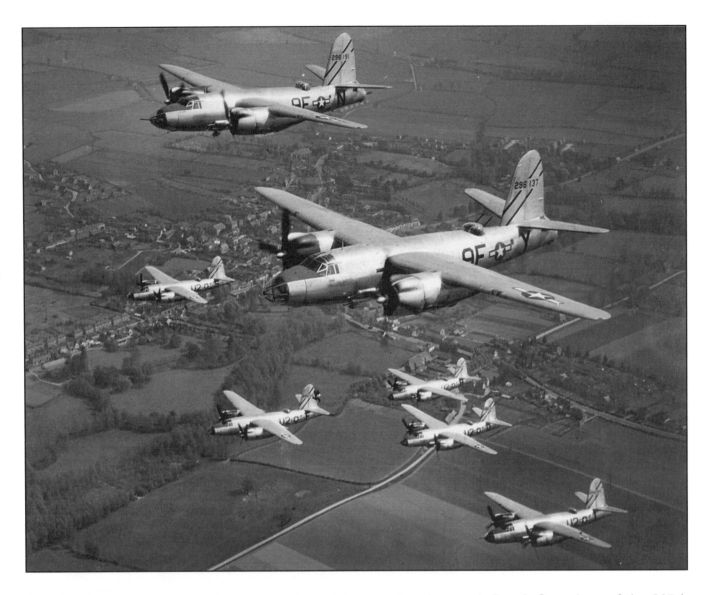

The fuselage letters 9F on these silver B-models indicates the 597th Bomb Squadron of the 397th Bomb Group. Diagonal group marking on tail is yellow. The aircraft were depicted over England sometime in 1944 before the unit moved onto the Continent that August. (AAF)

thirds of the production of B-26Fs, amounting to 200 of 300 F-models, were transferred to the Royal Air Force and the South African Air Force as the Marauder III, carrying serials HD402 through HD601. The last production variant, the B-26G, resulted in 150 Marauders of this type being delivered to the RAF with serials HD602 through HD751 running contiguously from the first batch of Marauder IIIs; in fact, these G-models were also called Marauder III.[18]

Royal Air Force squadrons operating the Marauder included Nos. 14, 39, 326, 327, and 454. In the South African Air Force, Marauders served in squadrons 12, 21, 24, 25, and 30. Crews from Canada, Australia, and Greece also flew Marauders at some time. The other large-scale recipient of B-26s was France.

France in the Fracas

Free French combat pilots began serving the Allied cause as early

as the Tunisian campaign, although the AAF did not keep detailed records of French participation until October 1943. By that time, one French B-26 Marauder squadron was counted among 12 operational French squadrons. Mediterranean Allied Air Forces (MAAF) plans called for introducing French crews to combat "gradually with relatively easy patrol and convoy duties under Coastal Air Force and then to transfer them to Tactical Air Force when their flying proficiency was

such that they could profitably undertake offensive operations." The first Free French unit to make the transition was I/22 Squadron. It was also the first to receive B-26 Marauders. The unit joined the Mediterranean Allied Tactical Air Force (MATAF) in April 1944, with French General Bouscat participating in its first mission.[19]

The introduction of French units into MATAF was effective. According to an official MATAF history: "All were operated along AAF or RAF lines, flying the same formations, following Allied R/T procedure, etc. The system worked exceedingly well and the French squadrons dovetailed into MATAF to everyone's satisfaction." One MATAF official who observed French Marauder crews under the 42nd Wing readying for combat in March 1944 wrote to USAAF chief General Henry H. Arnold: "The French pilots average more flying time and are older and more experienced than our pilots in the 42nd Wing. They are most enthusiastic about the B-26."[20]

In the early summer of 1944, supplies of Marauders to French squadrons who were completing their training were lagging. According to MAAF, 46 B-26s needed to be earmarked for the French from Mediterranean Theater stocks shortly to avoid the prospect of having trained French squadrons languish without bombers. On 2 June 1944, General Arnold approved this diversion of AAF B-26s, with the aircraft given to the French to be replaced when the original French allotment arrived overseas.[21] (This may explain why some Free French B-26s carried French roundels superimposed over the bars of the AAF star-and-bars insignia.)

French Marauder crews were tasked to support the invasion of southern France in the summer of 1944. As French Marauder units began taking up residence in reclaimed portions of France, their control passed gradually from MAAF to USSTAF (United States Strategic Air Forces). During their tenure in MAAF, French B-26 Marauders served in the following units:

Sqd.	Assignment
I/22	NACAF (Oct. '43 – Mar. '44);
	MATAF (Apr. '44 – Oct. '44)
II/20	MATAF (Apr. '44 – Oct. '44)
I/19	MATAF (May '44 – Oct. '44)
II/52	MATAF (Aug. '44 – Oct. '44)
II/63	MATAF (Aug. '44 – Oct. '44)
I/32	MATAF (Sep. '44 – Oct. '44)

During their tenure with MAAF, French Squadrons I/22, II/20, and I/19 were associated with the 31st Group; II/52, II/63, and I/32 were associated with the 34th Group.[22]

Silver-bellied B-26G (43-34165) of the 391st Bomb Group came to grief on wet pavement on 2 December 1944. Triangle group identifier on tail was painted yellow. (AFHRA)

One a Day in Tampa Bay

Darkly catchy, the saying "one a day in Tampa Bay" was coined to describe, by exaggeration, the losses of B-26 Marauders due to training mishaps in Florida. If crashes involving green crews and hot, short-wing Marauders were attention-getting, the accident tally kept by the AAF offers some interesting points. The overall accident rate in the continental United States from 1942 to 1945 for Marauders was 55 per 100,000 flying hours. By comparison, the Douglas A-20 posted an overall accident rate in the United States of 131 per 100,000 flying hours, and the newer A-26 came in slightly worse than the Marauder at 57 accidents per 100,000 flying hours in the United States for the same time period. Of the aircraft types the AAF tracked individually, the Douglas C-54 transport was the safest in American skies, posting a wartime accident rate of 18 per 100,000 flying hours. The A-36 attack variant of the Mustang was highest of all, at 274 mishaps reported per 100,000 flying hours. North American Aviation's B-25 Mitchell came in at 33 accidents per 100,000 flying hours in the United States.[23]

There was a demonstrable learning curve with the Marauder. As instructors gained more experience and were able to use the hindsight of others who had flown the Martin bomber, stateside mishap rates dramatically diminished. For 1942 through August 1945, Marauder mishaps in the United States were characterized by the AAF in a postwar statistical study:[24]

The decline in the B-26 accident rate is a remarkable indicator of the AAF's ability to tame the beast by learning its ways. The tempo of training operations is reflected in the fact that the number of B-26 accidents increased dramatically in 1943 and to a lesser extent in 1944 even as the rate per 100,000 flying hours plummeted.

B-26 Marauder Accidents in the United States

	1942	1943	1944	Thru 08/1945
Rate/100,000 hrs.	162	65	37	31
Accident Totals	165	304	195	75
Aircraft Wrecked	88	159	123	38
No. of Fatalities	249	382	280	82

When Marauders occasionally flew decoy missions to confuse German defenses while other formations, possibly of B-17s or B-24s, headed to strategic targets, the B-26s subsequently were sometimes emblazoned with duck mission symbols indicating their use as decoys. (Stuart Perrin family via Cam Martin)

---

[1] Memo, 1Lt. James P. Muri (18th Reconnaissance Squadron), to Commanding General, VII Bomber Command, Subject: "Report of Combat; B-26 Airplane A.P. #42-1391," 6 June 1942 (filed at AFHRA). [2] Memo, Lt. Col. Karl Truesdell, Jr., to CO, Air Force Ferrying Command, Foreign Wing, Subject: "Report of the Battle of Midway," 10 June 1942 (filed at AFHRA). [3] Memo, Capt. James F. Collins, Jr. (69th Bomb Squadron), to Commanding General, VII Bomber Command, Subject: "B-26 in Battle of Midway," 6 June 1942 (filed at AFHRA), and Memo, Lt. Col. Karl Truesdell, Jr., to CO, Air Force Ferrying Command, Foreign Wing, Subject: "Report of the Battle of Midway," 10 June 1942 (filed at AFHRA). [4] Memo, Lt. Col. Karl Truesdell, Jr., to CO, Air Force Ferrying Command, Foreign Wing, Subject: "Report of the Battle of Midway," 10 June 1942 (filed at AFHRA). [5] Memo, Capt. James F. Collins, Jr. (69th Bomb Squadron), to Commanding General, VII Bomber Command, Subject: "B-26 in Battle of Midway," 6 June 1942 (filed at AFHRA). [6] Memo, 1Lt. James P. Muri (18th Reconnaissance Squadron), to Commanding General, VII Bomber Command, Subject: "Report of Combat; B-26 Airplane A.P. #42-1391," 6 June 1942 (filed at AFHRA). [7] Report, *The Air Force in North Africa,* HQ 12th Air Force, October 1943. [8] *Ibid.* [9] *Ibid.* [10] *Ibid.* [11] *Ibid.* [12] *Ibid.* [13] *Ibid.* [14] *Ibid.* [15] Bob Considine, "B-26 Reforms—and What a Ship It Is Now!," Washington Post, 10 October 1943. [16] William Green, *Famous Bombers of the Second World War,* Hanover House, Garden City, New York, 1959. [17] *Ibid.* [18] *Ibid.* [19] "MAAF History of French Air Force," circa May 1945 (filed at AFHRA). [20] *Ibid.* [21] *Ibid.* [22] *Ibid.* [23] *Army Air Forces Statistical Digest, World War II,* Office of Statistical Control, HQ, USAAF, December 1945. [24] *Ibid.*

Seldom were World War II bomber crews photographed inflight with this clarity. Head-on angle emphasizes the slightly out-of-round accommodation the fuselage cross section made for the cockpit canopy. One flexible and one fixed .50-caliber machine gun are clearly visible in the nose. (Merhar/AFHRA)

Marauder at left of photo received punishing flak burst that ultimately resulted in the death of the bombardier after he was able to release bombs; a gunner was also injured. The aircraft was from the 323rd Bomb Group on a mission over Dieppe. (AAF via National Archives)

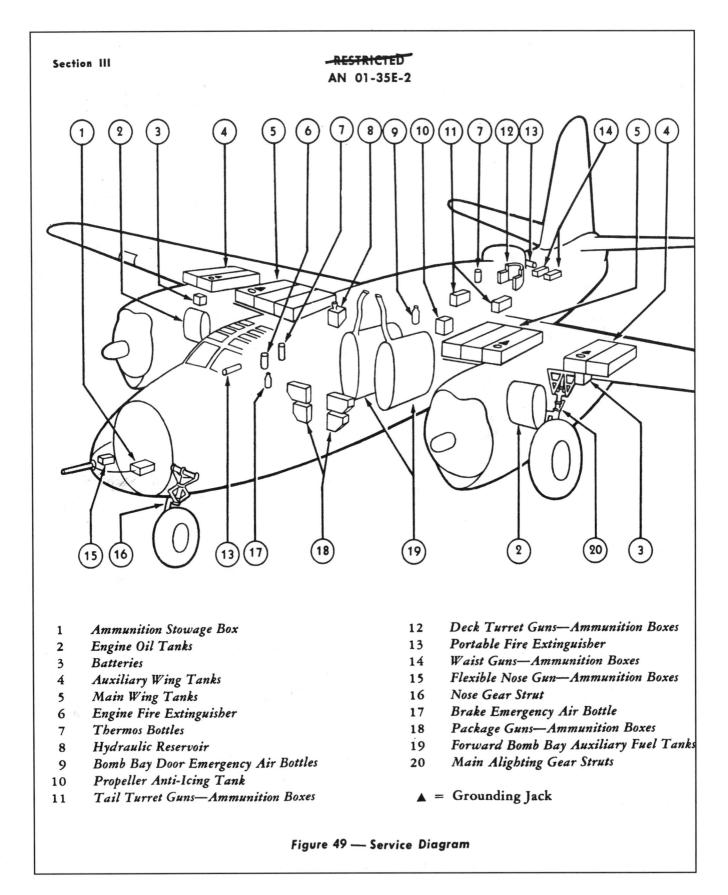

1   Ammunition Stowage Box
2   Engine Oil Tanks
3   Batteries
4   Auxiliary Wing Tanks
5   Main Wing Tanks
6   Engine Fire Extinguisher
7   Thermos Bottles
8   Hydraulic Reservoir
9   Bomb Bay Door Emergency Air Bottles
10 Propeller Anti-Icing Tank
11 Tail Turret Guns—Ammunition Boxes

12 Deck Turret Guns—Ammunition Boxes
13 Portable Fire Extinguisher
14 Waist Guns—Ammunition Boxes
15 Flexible Nose Gun—Ammunition Boxes
16 Nose Gear Strut
17 Brake Emergency Air Bottle
18 Package Guns—Ammunition Boxes
19 Forward Bomb Bay Auxiliary Fuel Tanks
20 Main Alighting Gear Struts

▲ = Grounding Jack

Figure 49 — Service Diagram

Marauder phantom view depicted ammunition boxes, fluid tanks, and other features of the B-26 requiring servicing or filling. (Frederick A. Johnsen Collection)

Strike camera recording the bomb release on a 391st Bomb Group mission captured the lethal drama as bombs from one B-26 knocked an engine off a Marauder, which then banked and collided with another B-26 which lost its aft fuselage and plunged to Earth as well. (AAF)

Photographed from both sides, a 323rd Bomb Group Marauder lost its left engine and began a flaming descent. (Al Lloyd Collection)

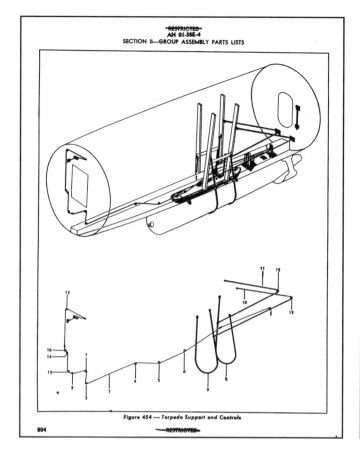

Figure 454 — Torpedo Support and Controls

804

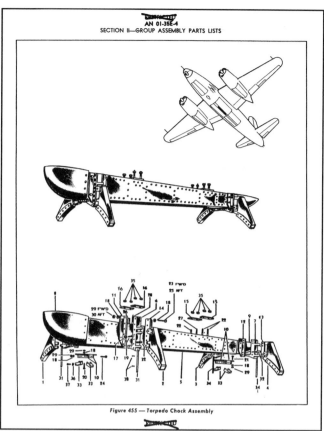

Figure 455 — Torpedo Chock Assembly

Artwork from a Marauder illustrated parts book showed a torpedo in place with two cables securing it. The cables passed through holes in the closed bomb bay doors. (Frederick A. Johnsen Collection)

A tapered external torpedo chock, or mount, could be affixed to some early Marauders between the forward bomb bay doors. The torpedo was angled nose down when installed. (Frederick A. Johnsen Collection)

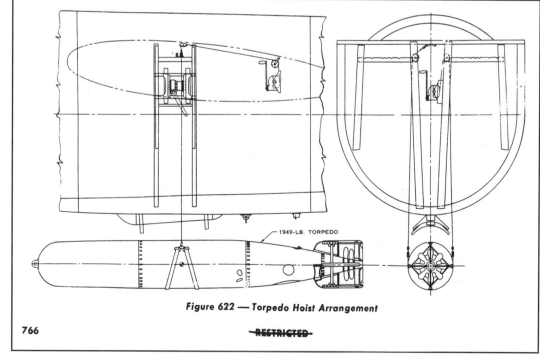

Diagrams from a B-26 erection and maintenance manual showed how to winch a Mark XIII Model 1 torpedo in place. (Frederick A. Johnsen Collection)

1949-LB. TORPEDO

Figure 622 — Torpedo Hoist Arrangement

766

MARTIN
B-26 MARAUDER

French wartime Marauders sometimes had individual aircraft numbers painted on top of their serials; French tricolor fin flashes of these Marauders are on the rudder, not the fixed vertical fin as was British practice. (AAF/National Archives)

Little Sirocco *gave the 319th Bomb Group at least 117 sorties.* (Frederick A. Johnsen Collection)

A formation of French B-26s carried the war to German forces occupying parts of southeast France in 1944. (AAF/National Archives)

Marauders of the 12th Air Force's 319th Bomb Group made one of their celebrated six-ship simultaneous takeoffs from a large North African airfield in 1943. The broad airfield allowed the Marauders to form up more quickly and head to the target sooner than if they had to rely on single-ship takeoffs. (Frederick A. Johnsen Collection)

The crew of Dragon Wagon emblazoned both sides of its Marauder with the name, and the right side with a depiction of the beast as well as 31 mission markers when the photos were taken. (Fred LePage Collection)

Ninth Air Force Marauder, probably from the 391st Bomb Group, showed results of severe tail damage that ripped off the top of the vertical fin and left the torn rudder's top hinge in a shambles. Plexiglas tail gunner's canopy has been removed. (AAF)

WARBIRD**TECH**
SERIES

TRUE COLORS

The silver bullet finish of the first B-26 gave way to olive drab uppers and gray undersurfaces quickly even before America entered World War II. A B-26 Dash-2 erection and maintenance manual specified the olive drab upper surfaces should have an irregular demarcation line "where the tangent makes an angle of 60 degrees with the horizontal. Blend line uniformly with spray gun." The olive region included the area directly under the high-mounted wings. The tech order also called for the use of olive drab on "reflecting surfaces in bombardier's compartment (nose ring, gun mount casting, seat, front face of frame, etc.)." Curtiss Electric prop spin-ners were to be painted olive drab, too. Nose and main gear were to be given the neutral gray color of the undersurfaces of camouflaged B-26s. Marauders destined for the Royal Air Force were to receive standard AAF camouflage instead of British variations.

With the advent of natural metal finish (NMF) Marauders, Alclad aluminum and 2S, 3S, and 52S aluminum did not require painting. Other aluminum alloys were to be painted first with a coat of zinc chromate primer then topped with two coats of aluminum lacquer. When olive drab upper surfaces were deleted from Marauders at the factory, the AAF tech order specified a patch of olive drab be retained ahead of the pilots' windscreen.

This U.S. Navy JM photographed at the Martin airfield had an operational-style tri-color camouflage scheme seldom seen on Marauders. (Martin/Charles Cignatta via Stan Piet)

Natural metal finish gave this B-26G-5MA (43-34396) a silver bullet appearance. The decision to delete camoflauge from Marauders in production was somtimes altered in the field. (Martin/Charles Cignatta via Stan Piet)

Musee de L'Air's refurbished B-26G was photographed during its movement from the restoration facility to the museum on 30 July 1998. Like some late-war Ninth Air Force Marauders, this example has natural metal side and lower surfaces and camouflaged upper surfaces. (Laurent Boulestin)

The Terre Haute Tornado, a B-26B (42-95906) showed wear-and-tear as well as replacement parts when photographed in England circa 1944-45. White triangle on tail indicated the 344th Bomb Group, Ninth Air Force. (Brown/USAFA)

WARBIRD**TECH**
S E R I E S

Details on the cockpit section of the B-26B *Flak Bait* (41-31773) displayed in the National Air and Space Museum include red emergency handles atop the canopy and yellow seat cushions inside the cockpit. (Frederick A. Johnsen Collection)

Two men extend a red target sleeve on the ramp near a pair of U.S. Navy JM-1s at a stateside naval air station. Yellow aircraft is BuAer No. 66713. (U.S. Navy)

Busy wartime ramp hosted a bright yellow JM-1 and a taxiing Royal Air Force Marauder III (HO545, ex-B-26F 42-96472), in front of a Stinson 105 and a Navy PBJ Mitchell. (Martin/Charles Cignatta via Stan Piet)

The 344th Bomb Group, at airfield A-59 in France on 13 February 1945, logged its 200th mission when the photo was taken. (Jack Havener via Stan Piet)

A red tow target was mounted to a natural-metal JM-1 (66624) at Naval Air Station Norfolk, Virginia, during December 1943. (U.S. Navy via the National Archives)

MARAUDERS 5 FOR TRAINING

The duration of World War II caused a need for a variety of airframes for training purposes. In the United States, some B-26s served as trainers for new Marauder aircrews, while others towed target sleeves for aerial gunners.

AT-23 and TB-26

During 1943, the AAF stripped a number of B-26s of operational equipment, substituting tow target reels and gear. This resulted in 208 B-26Bs converted to AT-23A nomenclature, and 350 B-26Cs listed as AT-23Bs. Later, these designations were simplified as TB-26B and TB-26C. During production of G-model Marauders, 57 new aircraft were delivered in TB-26G configuration.

JM-1 and JM-2

The U.S. Navy and Marines operated trainer/target tug Marauders as the JM-1 (equivalent to the AT-23B/TB-26C) and as the JM-2 (erstwhile TB-26Gs). Two hundred twenty-five of the former and 47 of the latter were designated. Bureau of Aeronautics numbers assigned to JM-1s were 66595 through 66794 and 75183 through 75207. BuAer numbers for JM-2s were 90507 through 90521, and 91962 through 91993.[1] Some JM-1Ps were modified from JM-1s, indicating a photographic capability. At least one Navy Marauder became a testbed mother ship for the experimental Gorgon rocket project.

Mastering the Marauder

(The following tips on Marauder operations were included in an RB-26, B-26A, and B-26B flight manual published in the spring of 1943.)

If flying the B-26 was a no-nonsense operation, teaching crews how to operate the Marauder was sometimes blunt and to the point. A flight manual for early Marauders warned pilots: "You are a dead pigeon if you try to escape from the open hatches in the top of the pilot's compartment *during*

The crumpled hulk of B-26B 41-17611 in Florida shows details of the early-style twin .50-caliber tail gun mount. (AAF)

flight. If the engine propellers don't get you, the vertical fin or stabilizer will."[2]

The proximity of two four-blade Curtiss Electric propellers could have other consequences, as the early Marauder manual warned: "Pilot's and copilot's sliding windows must be CLOSED AND LOCKED during take-offs and landings, as they might fall out into the propellers."

The Marauder held other secrets revealed to new crews in the RB-26, B-26A, and B-26B pilot's manual: "Extreme care must be exercised to stop pumping *into* the right or left main tanks after they are full, as the pressure generated by the electric or hand fuel pump is sufficient to burst the gasoline tank. To make matters

They didn't all end up in Tampa Bay; this B-26 issued billows of roiling smoke following its training crash on 10 February 1943. (AAF)

A fire guard stands watch beside B-26B 41-17611 in Florida, one of a stream of early Marauder training mishaps. (AAF)

more complicated, the gage for the right and left main fuel tanks on the pilot's instrument board is calibrated to 275 U.S. gallons maximum, but the tank will hold 360 U.S. gallons."[3] As described in this early manual the copilot's rudder pedals did not have braking features and could be stowed out of the way in flight.

In the event the nosewheel could not be lowered, pilots were instructed to retract the mains before attempting a landing: "The airplane is very well constructed along the under side of the fuselage, and will make a very nice belly landing. Crew members should not be in the nose, tail, or upper turret during landing or take-off. Do not attempt to land with the main gear down if the nose gear is up." However, if this could not be avoided, crews were told to place weight aft, pick a hard-surfaced runway, and hold the nose up as long as possible, using the brakes with caution to avert an abrupt noseover.[4]

With its high wing loading, the early short-wing Marauders were dicey performers if one engine failed during takeoff: "THIS AIR-PLANE CANNOT MAINTAIN FLIGHT ON ONE ENGINE WHEN THE LANDING GEAR IS DOWN," the pilot's manual advised. "Cut both throttles and hold a straight course into a landing directly ahead." The procedure further taught that if an engine failed after the Marauder attained an airspeed of 150 miles an hour indicated "and the landing gear [is] retracted (or retracting) takeoff might be continued. Apply plenty of rudder toward the running engine, and at the same time drop the wing with the running engine slightly below the horizontal. Feather propeller and close cowl flaps and oil cooler shutters on failing engine, and if wing flaps were used, raise them cautiously in several steps to avoid losing altitude. Always keep directional control even if you have to reduce power on [the] good engine and dive to maintain flying speed."

So critical was the early Marauder on one engine that if one powerplant failed during normal flight, the crew was instructed: "If necessary, bombs or bomb bay tanks may be salvoed and if over suitable terrain, crew members may bail out. Thus it might be possible to effect a safe landing instead of crashing with all the crew aboard."[5]

The early Marauder flight manual alluded to a fliers' trick that many B-24 pilots subscribed to: getting "on the step." The 1943 Marauder manual said: "To obtain maximum cruising performance (miles-per-gallon), first climb four or five hundred feet higher than cruising altitude,

The bending of all propeller blades indicates the props were turning when B-26B 41-17611 came to grief in Florida during wartime training. The violence of the accident evidently popped most of the top half of the Plexiglas nose free from the fuselage. (AAF)

then set throttles and propellers for desired power, and fly 'downhill' to the selected cruising altitude. By trimming the ship with some excess speed and allowing this speed to be lost gradually, it is often possible to obtain 5 to 10 miles per hour more speed with the same power setting than if the airplane is merely trimmed out when the desired altitude has been reached."

Under the heading of acrobatics, the early manual was succinct: "Do not execute any acrobatics." The edict against Marauder acrobatics included vertical banks and

any dives above 345 miles an hour at a weight of 28,800 pounds, or 325 miles an hour at 31,800 pounds. This RB-26, B-26A, and B-26B manual warned against getting these Marauders into a spin: "DO NOT SPIN THIS AIRPLANE, and so fly it that you do not get into attitudes from which spins might result. Recommended recover procedure: Ride with the spin without pressure on controls for about one-half turn, then briskly apply full opposite rudder followed with neutral stick and hold it there. When rotation stops, nose down and get at least 150 mph IAS [Indicated Airspeed]

before attempting to level off. Rotation may not stop immediately, so hold opposite rudder for 5 turns before attempting any other method of recovery. *There is, at present, no 'sure-fire' method of spin recovery for this airplane* [emphasis added]."[6]

In a full-flaps approach to landing at an airspeed of 150 miles an hour, the early Marauder handbook noted, "the descent is rather steep (approximately 45 degrees), but the airplane is easily leveled out for landing." The finesse required of Marauder pilots was evident on landing, as the early flight manual said: "Every attempt should be made to be flying straight in on the final approach before lowering landing gear or flaps; but if necessary to make turns after the gear and flaps have been lowered, the turns should be gentle and never require over a 15 degree bank." There were other landing perils: "Side slipping is extremely dangerous at low altitudes or during the approach for landing, as the engine on the low side is likely to cut out, and the airplane will not fly on <u>one</u> engine with the landing gear down." Further explanation of this side slip prohibition in the manual said: "… the fuel system will not supply adequate fuel to each engine."[7]

Center of gravity was crucial to good Marauder operations, and pilots were advised to use the aircraft's slide-rule load adjuster instrument to re-compute center of gravity after expending consumables: "If all bombs, ammunition, and fuel have been expended, the center of gravity will be too far forward for ease of control during landing. In such

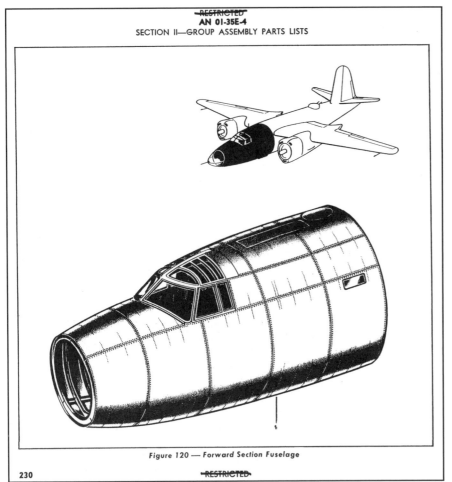

Figure 120 — Forward Section Fuselage

Curved skins of the forward fuselage made a tidy package of the Marauder cockpit, radio room, and bombardier's area, as depicted in a B-26 illustrated parts book. (Frederick A. Johnsen Collection)

WARBIRD**TECH**
SERIES

case crew members may be moved to the rear."[8] (Nose-heaviness was a problem; some training Marauders carried several hundred pounds of dead weight in the aft fuselage to maintain balance. In view of this, the attempt to move the top turret forward on at least one Marauder seems ill-advised.)

Ditching the Marauder called for decisions by the pilot before hitting the water, as delineated in the early B-26/A/B flight manual: "The pilot must insure that the bomb doors are opened, the bombs and containers dumped and the doors closed again. It takes approximately 30 seconds to open and close doors and, if there is any doubt that there is time to do this, it is better to keep the doors closed; in this case it is essential for the pilot to check that the bombs are SAFE.

"Lower hatches must be checked for security and upper ones dumped. Hatches may jam upon impact and it is important that the crew leave the ship without a moment's delay." Crews were told, in the case of night ditching, to dim interior lighting to enhance night vision, and once the aircraft was on the water, "all lights should be left on to facilitate search, in the event the airplane should float."[9]

The manual described the sequence of events in a B-26 ditching: "If the airplane alights tail down as it should, there will be a primary slight impact as the rear of the airplane strikes. This will be followed by a severe impact with quick stop in most cases. If the alighting has been made too fast, a bounce will occur. As the airplane comes to rest the nose will bury, but if the alighting has been carried out correctly, the effect of the nose burying will be minimized." Pilots were told to ditch on the upslope of a swell if making a crosswind approach along a swell. "In a steep swell, the pilot should ditch along the top of the swell unless there is a very strong crosswind. In ditching across the swell, the airplane should be put down on an upslope toward the top."

The descent rate of the Marauder could be lessened with any available power, as the early B-26

Natural-metal AT-23, given individual aircraft identification Z-141, ground to a halt on a collapsed right main gear at Las Vegas Army Airfield, Nevada, on 15 May 1944. AT-23s often provided target tug service for gunners in training. (AAF via Marty Isham)

One of the straight B-26s (40-1542) served in a training role, minus top turret, at Del Rio, Texas. In addition to wear-and-tear, the paint shows evidence of medium-green blotching to further camouflage the Marauder's silhouette. (McLaughlin/SDAM)

manual noted: "Use of power is advisable, as even one engine will aid in flattening out the approach. Care must be taken to keep ample rudder control at all times during descent." If possible, Marauder pilots were told, they should make a power-on ditching because it would make for a better descent path to the water: "The value of power in ditching is so great that the pilot should always ditch before fuel is quite exhausted, if it is certain that land cannot be reached." Once on the water, crews were told: "GET OUT FAST as this plane sinks quickly."[10]

Cold weather operations called for some special procedures by Marauder aircrews. "Following the take-off from snow or slush covered fields, operate landing gear, flaps, and bomb bay doors through a complete cycle two or three times to prevent freezing in their 'up' position," the RB-26/A/B flight manual explained. Other cold-weather precautions included: "Momentarily increase propeller speed by about 200 rpm every half-hour, to assure continued operation of the propeller governors. Return propeller to the desired cruising rpm. ... Operate power turret occasionally to keep it free. ... Stay on pre-

arranged flight course so searchers will be able to find you if you are forced down. Except in extreme emergency, it is better to land or crash-land than bail out. This airplane does a beautiful, safe, belly landing."[11]

Excess Short Wings

In the summer of 1944, when AAF Marauder inventory already had reached its zenith, Third Bomber Command voiced concerns about the B-26s it had in the United States for crew training, citing "an inadequate number of training aircraft and an excessive number of outmoded

short-wing B-26s." Short-wing Marauders were said to be more susceptible to runaway propellers because the electrical system had less capacity than on later B-26s. Additionally, the higher landing and stalling speeds of short-wing B-26s could cause dangerous situations for student fliers, especially when migrating from the slightly-more-benign long-wing variants.[12]

Through the summer of 1944, the AAF gleaned B-26s around the United States for use as trainers by Third Bomber Command in an effort to retire the short-wing B-26s from that role. The fortunes of war shifted by November, as the Third Bomber Command history reported, "requirements for B-26 crews dropped sharply, and the problem of the III Bomber Command became one of disposal of an excessive number of B-26 aircraft."

In August 1944, Third Bomber Command reported removing package guns and armor plate from B-26s "to adopt the airplanes to RTU [Replacement Training Unit] final-phase training and to insure more efficient single-engine operation. All aircraft receiving this modification were reclassified to 'TB' types."[13]

Training in Texas

By early 1944 student pilots at Laughlin Field, Del Rio, Texas, were flying some converted and lightened B-26s that the Laughlin Field history states were "designated as 'straight' AT-23s," evidently with no suffix model letter assigned. Laughlin also received some AT-23Bs in November and December 1943. The history fur-

Short-wing straight B-26 was photographed with its landing gear down, a configuration that demanded both engines be running to maintain altitude. (SDAM)

ther states big-wing B-26Bs used at the school were easier for students to fly than were early small-wing models.[14]

WASPs for Marauders

Members of the Women's Air Force Service Pilots (WASPs) program began training on Marauders at Dodge City Army Airfield, Kansas, on 14 October 1943. The base trained classes of WASPs from that date until graduating its last B-26 WASP class on 3 June 1944. In that time, 57 WASPs started the training and 39 finished it, while 18 of their compatriots were eliminated from the training, according to an official AAF history of the Dodge City WASP activity.[15]

During their intense nine-week training course at Dodge City, the WASPs got 75 hours of flying instruction on B-26s, divided into 30 hours of co-pilot time and 45 hours of first-pilot training. On top of this actual flying time, 20 hours in a Link trainer were provided. While learning to fly the demanding Marauder in 75 hours, the women spent 45 hours, including nine at night, in transition training, 20 hours on instruments, and 10 hours on navigation flights, including four hours at night. A Dodge City AAF history noted: "The course received by the WASPs is composed of that which is prescribed for officer students. Formation flying was the only phase of the regular training eliminated from the WASP program, and this phase was eliminated because the trainees had received no previous instruction in formation flying before reporting to this station."[16] Given the WASPs' frequent duties as ferry pilots and tow-target pilots, the lack of formation training was not an insurmountable obstacle to their mission effectiveness.

The AAF historical officer at Dodge City said the WASPs had more problems with technical training in ground school than did their male student officer counterparts. "However," the AAF historian noted, "this lack of technical background by the WASPs was overcome by the eagerness and determination to learn." The women finished ground school "with an average equal to that of student officers." One telling observation attributed to the Dodge City base's commanding officer noted, "… where these women pilots have voluntarily chosen transition training on the B-26, rather than being arbitrarily assigned this duty, that on the whole they have been more receptive to the training," than some of their male counterparts.[17]

[1] Peter M. Bowers and Gordon Swanborough, *United States Navy Aircraft Since 1911,* Putnam, London, 1976. [2] *Pilot's Flight Operating Instructions—RB-26, 26A and B-26B Airplanes,* HQ, Air Service Command, Patterson Field, Fairfield, Ohio, 5 March 1943, revised 25 April 1943. [3] *Ibid.* [4] *Ibid.* [5] *Ibid.* [6] *Ibid.* [7] *Ibid.* [8] *Ibid.* [9] *Ibid.* [10] *Ibid.* [11] *Ibid.* [12] "History of Headquarters III Bomber Command From 1 May to 31 December 1944, Vol. I, Narrative," Historical Division, HQ III Bomber Command, circa 1945. [13] *Ibid.* [14] "Station History of Army Air Forces Pilot School" (Specialized 2-Engine), Laughlin Field, Del Rio, Texas, circa February–March 1941 (filed at AFHRA). [15] Report, *History of the Women's Air Force Service Pilots Program—Dodge City Army Air Field, Dodge City, Kansas,* 7 December 1944 (filed at AFHRA). [16] *Ibid.* [17] *Ibid.*

Martin used this ramp for preflight instruction at its Marauder school, with a mix of short-tail and tall-tail versions evident. (AFHRA)

Forward fuselage furnishings in the B-26 included extension lights for the bombardier (part number 4) and for the pilots and radio compartment (number 2), as well as a desk lamp for the radio operator (part 7).
(Carl Sholl Collection)

AN 01-35E-4
SECTION 11—GROUP ASSEMBLY PARTS LISTS

Figure 314 — Forward Section Fuselage Electrical Equipment

Below: *At the Martin school, this Marauder (B-26 number 40-1423) airframe served as an electrical system troubleshooting training aid.*
(Frederick A. Johnsen Collection)

WASPs at Dodge City, Kansas, learned intricacies of their Marauders' R-2800 engines, circa 1944. (AAF)

Below: *Two crewmen in sheepskin flying gear and backpack parachutes loading an A-6A flag type towed target into a 12th Tow Target Squadron AT-23, circa March 1944. The 30-foot by six-foot target was reeled out by a C-5 windlass in the forward bomb bay. (AAF)*

An instructor at the Martin Marauder school explained engine operation to a student in one of the training B-26s. (AFHRA)

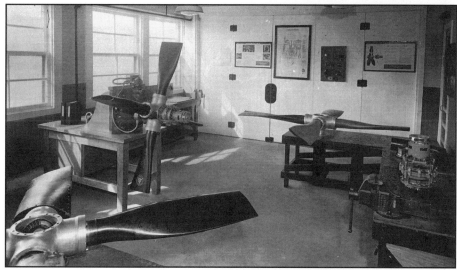

Truncated hollow Curtiss Electric B-26 propellers served as training aids at the Martin company school. (Martin/AFHRA)

A cowled R-2800 Marauder engine on a dolly revealed its accessory section at the Martin school. (Martin/AFHRA)

An AT-23 dragged a cloth A-6A target for the benefit of student gunners aboard a B-17 at Las Vegas Army Airfield, Nevada, circa 1943. (AFHRA)

Wearing Mae West life preservers as if to underscore the "One a Day in Tampa Bay" slogan, Marauder crews ambled among 21st Bomb Group operational training B-26s at MacDill Field, Florida. The convenience of top-opening canopy hatches was appreciated on hot airfields where the greenhouse effect under closed glazing was intense. (AAF)

POSTWAR MARAUDERS

The rapid withdrawal of Marauders from the USAAF following the end of World War II resulted in most of the remaining fleet being scrapped. A few B-26s entered American civilian use as executive transports and, in one instance, a cross-country racer, but in the main, the Marauder's career ended with the war. Scrapyards, including Kingman, Arizona; Sandia (Albuquerque), New Mexico; and Ontario, California, briefly hosted ramshackle Marauders before most were cut up.

Flak Bait, an honored combat veteran B-26B (41-31773) of the 322nd Bomb Group, survived combat and the postwar era by becoming part of the National Air and Space Museum's collection. The nose section was placed on display in the museum in Washington, D.C., with the rest of the airframe held in storage.

A B-26G (43-34581) is displayed at the U.S. Air Force Museum near Dayton, Ohio. Part of the French Air Force contingent, this G-model later served as a training aid for Air France employees before the Air Force Museum acquired it in June 1965.

The Musee de l'Air saved B-26G 44-68219 in Paris. Delivered to the French Air Force in May 1945, 68219 outlived most of its contemporaries as one of a trio of Marauders used for instructional purposes by Air France at Vilgenis, near Paris, beginning in the early 1950s. Into the 1960s, when one of the three was transferred to the U.S. Air Force Museum in Ohio, 68219 was earmarked for the Musee de l'Air. Restoration got underway in the 1990s, and the sole remaining French Marauder escaped a disastrous fire that destroyed a number of museum aircraft in storage. It was restored with markings representative of the French Groupe de Bombardement GB II/20, "Bretagne", 31st Escadre. The French B-26G was placed on display in 1998.[1]

For years, the Confederate Air

In postwar France, *B-26G 43-34584 was altered with jet inlets as a flying testbed for the Atar turbojet. Where once a .50-caliber machine gun had sprouted from the Plexiglas nose, a test instrumentation boom was substituted on this flying laboratory.* (Bowers Collection)

Force Museum nurtured a C-model Marauder (41-35071) through an ongoing process of restoration and overhaul. This aircraft was registered to United Airlines in 1946 as N5546N. Passing through a couple of southern California owners, N5546N was entered in the 1949 Bendix Trophy Race, under race number 24. In the mid-1950s, it was modified as an executive aircraft and alternately may have carried the registration N500T. After another series of short ownerships, by September 1961 B-26 41-35071 flew under Mexican civil registration XB-LOX, operated by Pemex, a petroleum company. Back in the United States by October 1965, the Marauder came into the collection of the Confederate Air

Force organization about two years later.[2] This Marauder suffered landing gear problems and spent much of the time on the ramp instead of flying until the last half of the 1980s when it was flown triumphantly. A crash subsequently destroyed the Confederate Air Force Marauder on 28 September 1995.

The other complete Marauder extant in the United States as of this writing is Kermit Weeks' straight B-26 model, serial 40-1464. One of three early-model B-26s recovered in a wilderness area of Canada in 1971 by pioneering warbird collector David Tallichet, 40-1464 and its sister ships 40-1501 and 40-1459, were dismantled and

shipped to Chino, California for reconstruction. The trio, assigned to the 42nd Bomb Group, had made forced landings in the face of low fuel and a snowstorm west of Fort Nelson, British Columbia, on 16 January 1942. Their intended destination was combat in the Aleutians; their fate was abandonment to the elements until they were retrieved almost 30 years later. The crews of all three Marauders, including the pilots of 40-1464 who were injured when its nose ruptured in the crash landing, were rescued within a week because P-40 pilots en route to Alaska performed a search of the area when the bombers went missing.[3]

Though it was impractical by

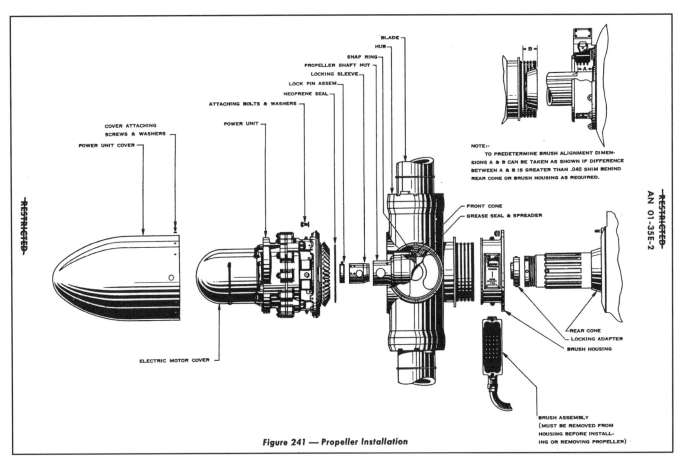

Figure 241 — Propeller Installation

Elongated propeller spinner (identified as "power unit cover" in the tech manual drawing) typified Curtiss Electric propeller assemblies. (Frederick A. Johnsen Collection)

The celebrated Flak Bait, *B-26B 41-31773 of the 322nd Bomb Group destined for preservation in the National Air and Space Museum of the Smithsonian Institution, was photographed in the lead of four Marauders over Europe. Letters "PN" on fuselage denote the 449th Bomb Squadron. (AAF)*

early World War II standards to remove the three B-26s, in the spring of 1942 the AAF sent an expedition to glean parts from the basically intact aircraft to keep others flying in the Aleutian campaign. By 1971, the scarcity of Marauders and a burgeoning interest in World War II aircraft made the three downed B-26s sufficiently interesting to prompt Tallichet's retrieval of them from the wilderness.

Because only 40-1464 had been landed gear down, it was deemed to be in the best overall condition even though its nosegear had col-lapsed during the landing. The damaged nose section of 1464 was replaced with the relatively intact nose from one of the other two Marauders, and Tallichet's restoration crews began a rebuilding process that spanned 20 years from April 1972 to April 1992, when, on the 18th of the month, 40-1464 made its first post-restoration test flight.

Trackers of warbird movements note the migratory nature of a percentage of the vintage aircraft fleet. In 1994 Tallichet sold some of his aircraft, including Marauder 40-1464 (civil registration N4297J), to Kermit Weeks in Florida. Following further restoration by Carl Scholl and Tony Ritzman's Aero Trader company at Chino, the short-wing Marauder made appearances at air shows including Sun 'n Fun in Florida and the giant Experimental Aircraft Association AirVenture at Oshkosh, Wisconsin.

The other two Million Dollar Valley B-26s are, as of this writing, reported to be the subject of long-term restorations, one (40-1459) intended to fly in Ohio; the other (using parts from 40-1501) to be static in upstate

New York. Evidently number 1501 surrendered many critical fuselage parts to the other two Marauders in the rescued trio, but the resourcefulness of warbird rebuilders has seen surprising Phoenix-like revivals of aircraft long thought gone.

A few other Marauders surfaced on the civilian registry after the war, including B-26C/AT-23B/JM-1 number 41-35373 operated by an air service in Charlotte, North Carolina in the late 1940s. Sister ship 41-35541 left the Navy to serve the National Advisory Committee for Aeronautics (NACA) by 1947, later entering the U.S. civil market as N75072. This aircraft may have been scrapped by the mid 1960s. A third B-26C/AT-23B/JM-1 (41-35542) was said to be used by Abrams Aerial Survey in Lansing, Michigan in the late 1940s. Following subsequent changes in ownership, this Marauder was given an executive conversion in Los Angeles by AirResearch circa 1953 for use by the Tennessee Gas Transmission Company of Houston, Texas. This Marauder was reportedly scrapped by the summer of 1965.[4]

Another C-model, 42-107640, variously registered N1501M, N66595, XH-100 (Honduras), and N1502, ran out of luck in a fatal crash near Marion, Ohio in July 1959. B-26C 42-107758, another sometime aerial survey and petroleum company Marauder, wound up under Mexican registration XB-PEX, where the aircraft crashed in Mexico City late in 1965.[5]

A few other Martin Marauders struggled in the postwar era, but their utility, and supportability, was eclipsed by more docile B-25s and other surplus types. Competency in combat was no guarantee of life in the postwar civilian market.

[1] From information by Laurent Boulestin. [2] John Chapman and Geoff Goodall, *Warbirds Worldwide Directory,* Warbirds Worldwide, Mansfield, England, 1989. [3] Paul Koskela, "'Million Dollar Valley' Marauder," *EAA Warbirds,* July 1998. [4] John Chapman and Geoff Goodall, *Warbirds Worldwide Directory,* Warbirds Worldwide, Mansfield, England, 1989. [5] *Ibid.*

Unarmed B-26C (41-35220) nearest camera may be one of many bombers converted to training purposes. Photographed at the Kingman, Arizona, scrapyard in 1947, this C-model carries the fuselage star in its aft location; the Marauder behind it has a forward-positioned star seen on some stateside B-26s. Extremely clean lines of the fuselage are emphasized on this unpainted and unarmed example. (Peter M. Bowers)

At one point during its long resurrection by the Confederate Air Force, the group's Marauder was photographed at Harlingen, Texas, with one engine and a three-blade propeller. (C. Mike Habermehl)

Peacetime was not kind to most Marauders; these stateside B-26s were scrapped at Oxnard, California. Once their R-2800 engines were removed, the airframes rocked back on their tails. Photos of non-combat B-26s sometimes show larger fuselage star insignia positioned farther forward than on typical combat Marauders. (A.U. Schmidt Collection via Peter M. Bowers)

Range cattle wandered among rows of silent Marauders in the Arizona desert at Kingman after the war. Thousands of Army Air Forces aircraft were scrapped and melted down at Kingman. By 1948, the Air Force had declared its few remaining Marauders obsolete. (William T. Larkins)

Back on its gear, David Tallichet's short wing Marauder was photographed early in its rebuilding process at Chino, California, on 29 December 1972. (Kenneth G. Johnsen)

WARBIRD**TECH**
SERIES

ARMING THE MARAUDER

The B-26 needed guns to protect itself from enemy fighters. But guns were a necessary evil on the Marauder; a weight-laden concession to the realities of aerial warfare. On 21 September 1942, Brig. Gen. E. L. Eubank, AAF director of bombardment, directed a standardized complement of guns be placed on Marauders as soon as possible. Eliminating light .30-caliber machine guns which had been used in some locations on early B-26s, General Eubank's edict called for one fixed and one flexible forward firing .50-caliber machine gun in the nose; four removable package gun pods with forward-firing .50-calibers on the side of the fuselage; two flexible waist .50-caliber weapons; and a tail turret with a pair of .50-calibers. At that time, General Eubank called off development of wing guns for the Marauder, possibly to the relief of wing vendor Goodyear.[1]

Martin Top Turret

Not surprisingly, the Marauder used Martin's own electrically-operated twin-gun top turret to guard the bomber's upper hemisphere — the first such installation of this power turret. This highly successful gun turret was ultimately adapted for use on a variety of bombers, including the Consolidated B-24 Liberator and PB4Y-2 Privateer, Lockheed Ventura and Harpoon variants, some

Heavily armed B-model was photographed over Europe after D-Day. Bi-fold bomb bay doors are open revealing a bomb; hydraulic M-6 tail gun mount affords protection from rear fighter attacks; open waist hatch accommodates a .50-caliber gun able to sweep low side approaches to the bomber. At the time of this photo, black-and-white invasion stripes included the top of the fuselage, a marking removed later in 1944 even while some undersurfaces retained the characteristic Allied identification striping. (AAF via Bowers Collection)

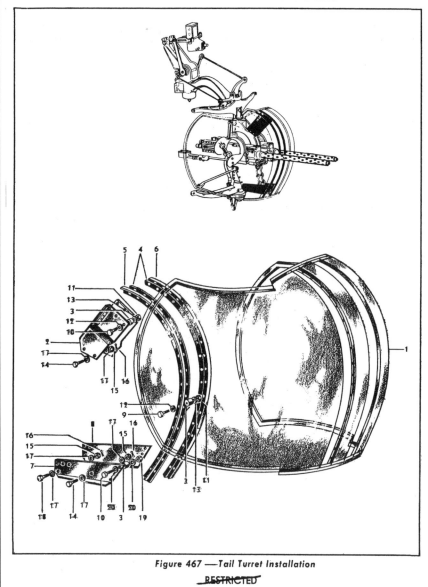

Figure 467 — Tail Turret Installation

RESTRICTED

As drawn for a B-26 illustrated parts book, a bulbous Plexiglas tail cap enclosed twin .50-caliber machine guns on Marauders beginning during B-model production. Heart of the gun emplacement was a hydraulic Bell M-6 or M-6A twin gun mount. (Carl Scholl Collection)

Lancasters, and into the postwar era aboard P2V Neptunes.

The Martin 250CE series top turrets were given the AAF designation A-3 with differentiating suffix letters; some versions were labeled A-14 in the AAF. The A-3 was used on the B-26A; the A-3A was put in the B-26B; the A-3C was used in the B-26 series, and the A-14 was designated for Marauder service, but superseded by the A-3C.[2]

The Marauder's upper turret was placed just aft of the rear bomb bay and forward of the waist guns. The turret featured a drop seat, so the gunner hoisted himself into position and brought the seat bottom up to latch in place beneath him. Operation of the turret was largely intuitive, with two grips to rock fore and aft for elevation and depression, or to simultaneously push and pull on opposite sides to effect lateral travel of the turret. The amount of pressure or displacement applied to the grips dictated the speed of turret movement. According to the AAF "Dash-One" pilot's manual, the guns could be moved diagonally by combining both azimuth and elevation movements through the grips. Both grips contained triggers; pulling either trigger would fire both guns.[3]

The guns could be elevated to 85 degrees overhead, and swept a full 360 degrees in azimuth, with fire interrupter cams protecting the vertical tail of the Marauder by opening the electrical gun firing circuits to cause gunfire to cease if the guns were aimed at the tail.[4]

It was possible to set the turret fire interrupters to allow both guns to fire if they straddled the vertical fin, although armorers were cautioned not to let clearances diminish below three inches. Even the seemingly stiff wing of the B-26B and C flexed upward as much as 6.8 inches under flight loads at the tip when carrying a full bomb load and half fuel. The propeller hub deflected upward 1.25 inches, according to an AAF Martin top turret manual, and these mea-

surements had to be taken into account when setting fire interrupters to miss the Marauder's propeller arcs by four inches.[5]

Waist Guns

Marauder waist guns were located below the horizon on each side of the aft fuselage. Each waist window mounted a single .50-caliber M-2 machine gun. Some B-26s had provision for a ventral tunnel gun installation. Early B-26s sometimes included flexible .30-caliber guns in their armament complement, although this was later standardized with longer-reaching .50-caliber weapons.

A curious recommendation in the B-26 mock-up report of 20 November 1939 called for the placement of "two Plexiglas openings with ball and socket gun mounts for caliber .50 machine guns ... in the rear bomb bay... . These gun positions shall be so designed as to best defend forward fire under the belly of the airplane." In reality, neither the aft bomb bay nor any meaningful form of ventral gun emplacements were ever very useful on the Marauder.[6]

Marauder waist guns came under scrutiny in a Third Bombardment Wing report dated 3 January 1943, based on tests with a B-26B. The Wing report was not charitable to Marauder waist gun field of fire at any altitude, but especially at low-level. The report documented the Wing's efforts to assimilate RAF experience at low-level bombing in an effort to find a niche for the Marauder in the European Theater of Operations (ETO) before the Eighth Air Force

57"
APPROX.

MOUNT—GUN
ARMY TYPE M-6

NAMES: Gun mount   Bell turret   Hydraulic gun mount   Hydraulic swivel gun mount

(Continued on page 71)   (RESTRICTED)

The M-6 twin-gun tail stinger on the Marauder, along with its linked gunsight, was located aft of armor that protected the gunner. Grips commanded hydraulic variable displacement pumps responsible for traversing and elevating the guns. (Bill Miranda Collection)

actually sent B-26s into combat later that year.[7] The Wing report made a prediction that would have chilling implications later: "We came to the conclusion that employment of the B-26 in the European Theater is limited apparently ... to daylight, zero-feet formations or low-altitude intruder missions with cloud cover." Once the Third Bomb Wing concluded the Marauder's war should be fought at low level, their report said the B-26 could be

Figure 464 — Waist Gun Installation
RESTRICTED

Low-mounted Marauder waist guns featured a swing-out arm mounting a fork that engaged an E-11 recoil adapter holding a .50-caliber machine gun. A flexible stainless-steel chute carried ammunition from a high-mounted 240-round box to the gun. (Frederick A. Johnsen Collection)

improved by deleting the waist and tunnel guns and gunner, for a savings of about 640 pounds around Station 475, resulting in a more favorable weight and balance for the B-26B.

"Since neither of the [B-26B] waist guns will fire above the horizontal, then with only a restricted lateral range, it is not believed that either of these guns will result in much added protection on low-level flights, certainly not to a sufficient extent to offset the disadvantage of that much weight at the position. The weight difference at Station 475 will add immeasurably to the performance of the airplane," the report explained.[8]

In practice, early low-level bombing over Europe was a disaster for Marauders, and waist guns were retained for use at the higher altitudes favored for the B-26.

Tail Guns

When Martin engineers were firming up the design of the B-26 in the fall of 1939, the decision to use a single vertical fin instead of the earlier-proposed twin tail had a side benefit, according to an AAF study: "Fairing for single tail would provide more head room for the rear gunner."[9]

The tail gun emplacement of the Marauder evolved during production, eventually incorporating a Bell hydraulically-boosted mount to facilitate swinging the weapons. The straight B-26 carried a single .30-caliber tail gun; the A-model increased firepower to a single .50-caliber in the tail. The B-26B introduced a pair of .50-calibers that could be fired individually by depressing only one trigger at a time.[10]

The B-26B-10 introduced a hydraulically-boosted tail gun emplacement with revised fuselage and window contours.[11] The Bell M-6 boosted tail unit used a clear Plexiglas cap through which the guns protruded; above this, the gunner's rear window was revised in shape. The boosted guns had a 90-degree cone of fire behind the Marauder. The unit used an N-8 gunsight placed about 17.5 inches above the gun mount. (A few early versions incorporated the Navy Mark 9 illuminated sight instead.) A mechanical linkage coordinated and moved the sight as the guns were moved by the operator. The guns could be moved as fast as 35 degrees per second with the

boosted unit. The gunner had armor plate between him and the guns.[12]

Package Guns

The demonstrated need for more forward strafing firepower on medium bombers led to the installation of four .50-caliber machine guns, two per side, mounted in aluminum "packages" on the fuselage near the nose. With Marauders in the European Theater often bombing at altitudes above strafing height, pilots occasionally activated the package guns in an effort to discourage frontal fighter attacks, although the efficacy, and frequency, of this tactic are not known.

Nose Guns

A flexible as well as fixed .50-caliber nose gun installation was available on B-26s. The flexible gun (in an E-11 recoil adapter and C-19 bracket) attached to a K-4 eyeball socket in the apex of the nose Plexiglas. Ammunition for this gun was stowed under the bombardier's seat on early B-26s.[13]

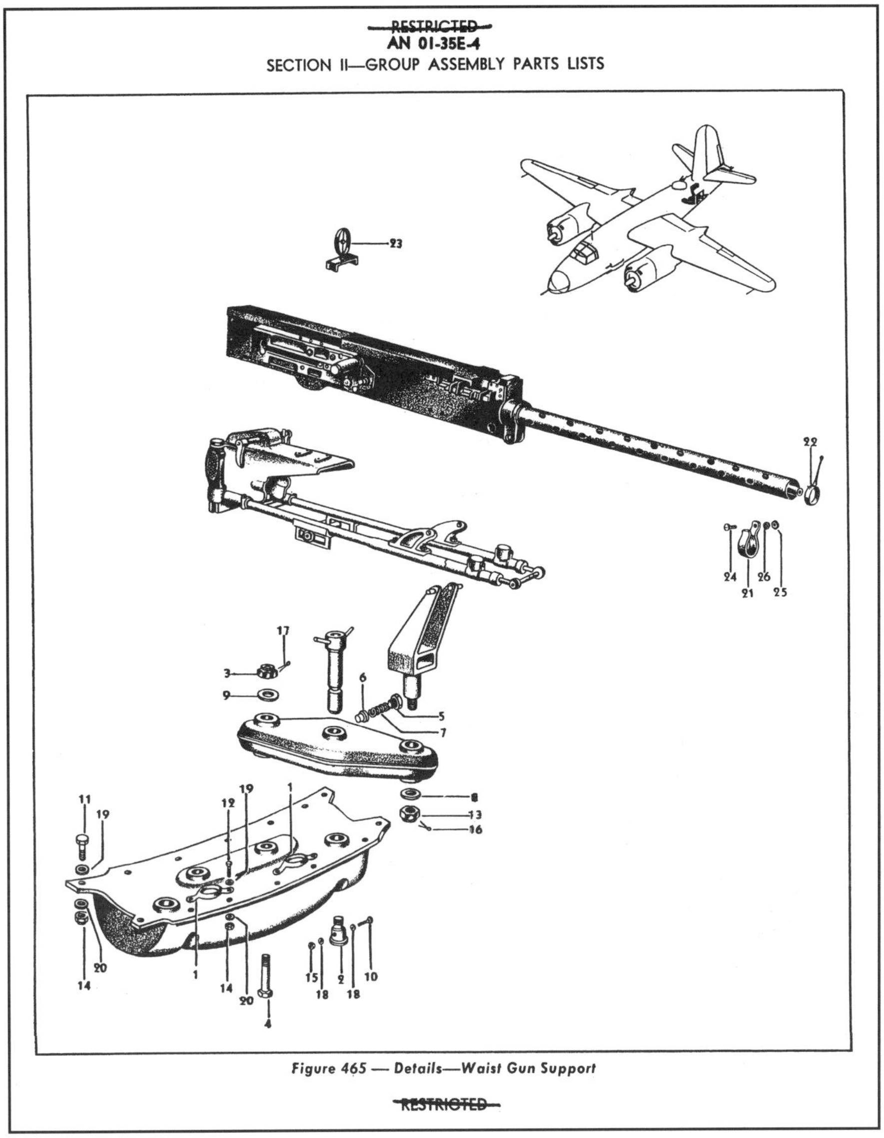

Bombsight Window

Martin designers went to great lengths to preserve the purity of their cigar-shaped Model 179's streamlining. An early proposed nose configuration involved a movable curved cover for the flat optical glass bombardier's window, envisioned as a means to help the bomber achieve its high top-speed potential by avoiding the flat pane's asymmetry. Following a 16 November 1939 inspection of the Martin mock-up, the service's mock-up board list-

Figure 465 — Details—Waist Gun Support

RESTRICTED

Detailed components of a Marauder waist gun set-up included a clip (part number 21 in the drawing) for stowing the gun in the fuselage when not in use. Gunsight depicted (part numbers 22 and 23) is a ring-and-bead style. E-11 recoil adapter with twin grips was common to many World War II AAF bombers. (Frederick A. Johnsen Collection)

ed disadvantages to this novel nose. It would require additional mechanical devices to move the streamline window cover; the mechanical aspects conceivably might fall victim to icing; and this nose afforded reduced vision. The mock-up board recommended use of a molded Plexiglas nose with a flat optical window, which ultimately was adopted.[14]

Access to the Marauder's nose compartment, as described in the RB-26/A/B flight manual, called for entering the aircraft through the nosewheel well. "Then go through pilot's compartment under copilot's flight control column and forward through small entrance door to nose compartment." In-flight escape route for the bombardier was back through

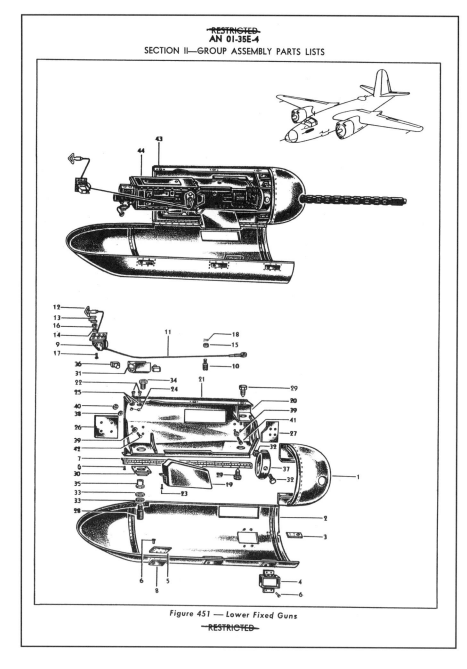

RESTRICTED
AN 01-35E-4
SECTION II—GROUP ASSEMBLY PARTS LISTS

Figure 451 — Lower Fixed Guns

RESTRICTED

Hinged cover allowed access to the .50-caliber machine gun in each B-26 package gun blister. Ammunition fed from inside the fuselage. (USAF via Dave Menard)

the pilot's compartment and out the forward bomb bay; on the ground, the bombardier could either exit via the nosewheel well or the overhead cockpit hatches.[15]

Bombs

Packing an internal bomb load typically between 3,000 and 4,800 pounds (depending on model and range) the Marauder underwent some fine-tuning to best serve its crews. For British variants as well as those flown by USAAF crews in the Middle East, India, and the Southwest Pacific, where some interaction with British ordnance was likely, B-26s were supposed to be modified to allow carriage of 1,000-pound British bombs slung beneath modified B-9 shackles; these Marauders also were to be made compatible with British nose and tail bomb fuse controls.[16] (Photos of AAF bombers in North Africa occasionally show British bombs dropping from their bays, evidence that American bombers could use British ordnance.)

Torpedoes

The Martin B-26 could carry a torpedo, an attribute the AAF tried to exploit early in the war. A 19 January 1942 report from the Naval Torpedo Station, Newport, Rhode Island, said flight tests were made

[1] *Case History of B-26 Airplane Project,* Air Force Materiel Command History Office, 22 February 1945. [2] Technical Order No. 11-1-64, *Index of Army-Navy Aeronautical Equipment—Armament,* AAF, 10 June 1944. [3] Technical Order No. 01-35EA-1, *RB-26, 26A, and B-26B Airplanes—Pilot's Flight Operating Instructions,* AAF, 5 March 1943, revised 25 April 1943. [4] *Ibid.* [5] Handbook of Overhaul Instructions AN 11-45BB-2, *Electric Power Operated Turrets—Type A-3C,* AAF, et al, 25 August 1943. [6] Excerpt from Air Corps B-26 Mock-Up Report, 20 Nov. 1939. [7] Memo, Maj. Jack E. Caldwell, Operations Officer, Third Bombardment Wing, to Colonel Anderson, Subject: "Modification of B-26B," 3 January 1943. [8] *Ibid.* [9] *Case History of B-26 Airplane Project,* Air Force Materiel Command History Office, 22 February 1945. [10] Technical Order No. 01-35EA-1, *RB-26, 26A, and B-26B Airplanes—Pilot's Flight Operating Instructions,* AAF, 5 March 1943, revised 25 April 1943. [11] Gordon Swanborough and Peter M. Bowers, *United States Military Aircraft since 1908,* Putnam, London, 1971. [12] Technical Order No. 11-1-64, *Index of Army-Navy Aeronautical Equipment—Armament,* AAF, 10 June 1944. [13] Technical Order No. 01-35EA-1, *RB-26, 26A, and B-26B Airplanes—Pilot's Flight Operating Instructions,* AAF, 5 March 1943, revised 25 April 1943. [14] *Case History of B-26 Airplane Project,* Air Force Materiel Command History Office, 22 February 1945. [15] *Pilot's Flight Operating Instructions—RB-26, 26A and B-26B Airplanes,* HQ, Air Service Command, Patterson Field, Fairfield, Ohio, 5 March 1943, revised 25 April 1943. [16] *Case History of B-26 Airplane Project,* Air Force Materiel Command History Office, 22 February 1945. [17] *Ibid.*

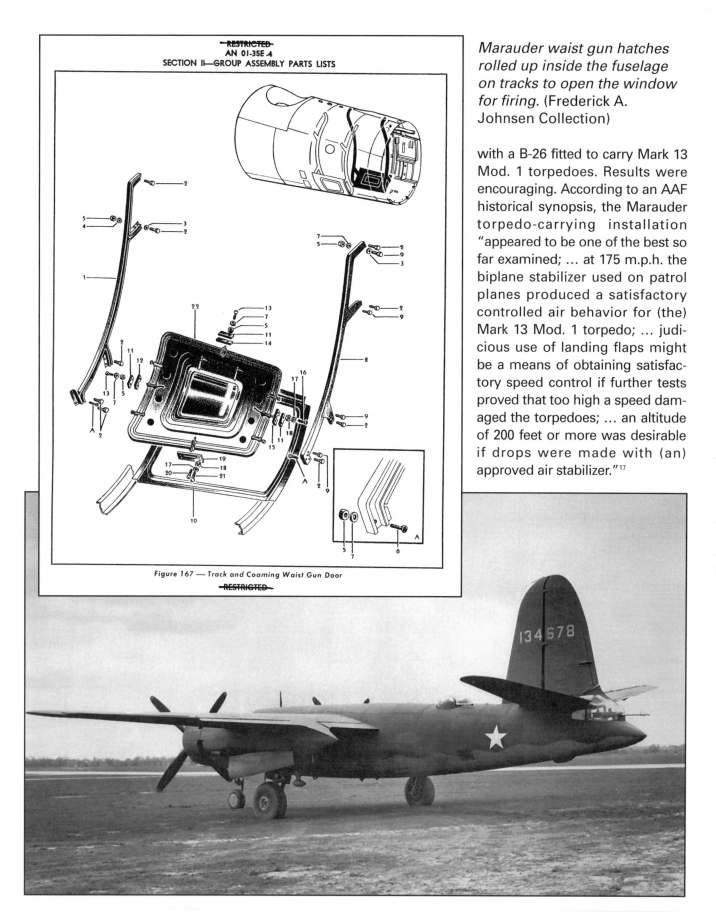

Figure 167 — Track and Coaming Waist Gun Door

Marauder waist gun hatches rolled up inside the fuselage on tracks to open the window for firing. (Frederick A. Johnsen Collection)

with a B-26 fitted to carry Mark 13 Mod. 1 torpedoes. Results were encouraging. According to an AAF historical synopsis, the Marauder torpedo-carrying installation "appeared to be one of the best so far examined; ... at 175 m.p.h. the biplane stabilizer used on patrol planes produced a satisfactory controlled air behavior for (the) Mark 13 Mod. 1 torpedo; ... judicious use of landing flaps might be a means of obtaining satisfactory speed control if further tests proved that too high a speed damaged the torpedoes; ... an altitude of 200 feet or more was desirable if drops were made with (an) approved air stabilizer."[17]

B-26C-5-MO (41-34678) shows twin .50-caliber tail guns extending above a pointed tail cap. (SDAM)

Seen through the propeller arc of another B-26, this Marauder appears to carry the short-lived torpedo mount beneath the bomb bay. (SDAM)

Moments before bomb release, a Marauder over Europe was photographed with the forward bomb bay in use. (AAF)

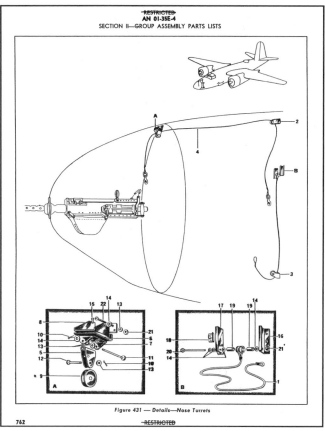

Figure 431 — Details—Nose Turrets

Crewmen beside the 387th Bomb Group's Pugnacious Peggy *provide a sense of scale. A pair of .50-caliber package guns is behind the crewman standing outside the aircraft. Pilot's armor plate attached outside the fuselage is visible by the highlights and shadows its thick edges create.* Pugnacious Peggy *was a B-26B-55 (42-96179) assigned to the Group's 558th Bomb Squadron. The crew included Stuart Perrin, pilot; Bill Bustard, copilot; Ole Olsen, radio operator/waist gunner; Elrod Larned, engineer/turret gunner; Frank Paden, bombardier/nose gunner; and Bob Norwood, tail gunner. (Stuart H. Perrin family via Cam Martin)*

Aluminum-reinforced Plexiglas B-26 noses were stockpiled in an Omaha, Nebraska warehouse for Marauder use during the war. (U.S. Army Signal Corps)

Cables clipped to the flexible Marauder nose gun helped balance its weight. Pouch beneath gun caught shells and links. (USAF via Dave Menard)

Snapshot of a crewman by the nose of B-26B *Gremlin* shows metal fairing around opening in the right lower nose Plexiglas for a fixed .50-caliber machine gun. (Stuart H. Perrin family via Cam Martin)

Before production, Martin toyed with the idea of covering the flat optical glass bombsight window with a curved shroud when not in use, to preserve the nose's rounded contours. (Fred LePage Collection)

Early B-26 (40-1447) was photographed with torpedo in place beneath the closed bomb bay. (U.S. Navy)

WARBIRD**TECH**
S E R I E S

USAAF MARAUDER UNITS

First Pathfinder Squadron (Provisional): Operated blind-bombing Marauder Pathfinders for the benefit of Ninth Air Force B-26 formations.

Ninth Bomb Group: Included some Marauders along with B-17s and B-24s in its roster for stateside training and testing of equipment.

17th Bomb Group: Converted to B-26s in 1942 and moved to North Africa late that year.

21st Bomb Group: Stateside training unit; may have used Marauders on some submarine patrols over the Gulf of Mexico before disbanding in October 1943.

22nd Bomb Group: Flew some Marauder patrols off the west coast of the United States in December 1941 and January 1942; flew Marauder combat over New Guinea.

25th Bombardment Group (Reconnaissance): Served Eighth Air Force in a variety of weather recon and photographic mapping missions with diverse aircraft including some B-26s.

28th Bomb Group: Included B-26s in its varied roster between 1941 and 1943, operating in Alaska from February 1941 until after V-J Day.

38th Bomb Group: Included B-26s in its roster; participated in the Battle of Midway in June 1942.

40th Bomb Group: Used B-26s and B-17s for training and Caribbean patrols circa 1942 – 1943.

42nd Bomb Group: Activated 15 January 1941; used some B-26s in training; equipped with B-25 Mitchells for combat in the Pacific in 1943.

319th Bomb Group: Trained with B-26s in 1942 before moving to North Africa for the invasion in November. Later converted to B-25s circa November 1944.

320th Bomb Group: Took Marauders into North African combat with 12th Air Force in April 1943.

322nd Bomb Group: Flew early disastrous low-level Marauder sorties for Eighth Air Force in May 1943; later assigned to Ninth Air Force in October 1943.

323rd Bomb Group: Activated in August 1942; flew Marauders for Eighth, and then Ninth, Air Forces.

335th Bomb Group: Served as a Third Air Force B-26 replacement training unit at Barksdale Field, Louisiana, from 1942 until it was disbanded on 1 May 1944.

336th Bomb Group: B-26 replacement training unit at various bases in Florida and Louisiana between 1942 and 1944.

344th Bomb Group: After service as a replacement training unit, moved to England and joined combat with Ninth Air Force in March 1944.

386th Bomb Group: Took Marauders to England for Eighth Air Force, flying first mission there in July 1943.

Assigned to Ninth Air Force in October 1943. Converted to Douglas A-26 Invaders late in the war.

387th Bomb Group: Activated 1 December 1942; moved to England with Eighth Air Force in June 1943, beginning combat missions that August. Transferred to Ninth Air Force in October 1943.

391st Bomb Group: Entered combat as a Ninth Air Force unit on 15 February 1944; began using Douglas A-26s by April 1945.

394th Bomb Group: Ninth Air Force Marauder unit that began combat in March 1944. On 9 August 1944, Capt. Darrell R. Lindsey of this group earned Medal of Honor for flying his stricken B-26 to a crash while affording his crew time to bail out.

397th Bomb Group: Moved to England in Spring of 1944, assigned to Ninth Air Force. Attacked V-weapon sites and coastal targets in advance of Normandy invasion, April – June 1944.

444th Bomb Group: Although listed as a Heavy bomb group, trained with B-26s as well as B-17s and B-24s in 1943, until redesignated a Very Heavy bomb group and assigned B-29s which it took into combat in 1944.

477th Bomb Group: Trained briefly with B-26s in 1943 while assigned to stateside Third Air Force.

(See also *Air Force Combat Units of World War II*, edited by Maurer Maurer, Office of Air Force History.)

SPECIFICATIONS

With a few caveats for model variations, the AAF Marauder erection and maintenance manual listed B-26 specifications and data intended to cover the B-26B-1-MA, B-26C-MO, B-26F-MA, B-26G-MA, and British Marauder II and III types. From that table the following characteristics are extracted:

Principal dimensions (aircraft in level flight position):

SPAN:	71 ft., 0 in.
LENGTH (overall):	56 ft., 6 in.
HEIGHT (top of fin):	21 ft., 6-3/8 in. *(B-26B-1 and C-models)*
	20 ft., 3 in. *(F- and G-models)*

Wing data:

AIRFOIL:	NACA 0017-64 (wing root)
	NACA 0010-64 Modified (wing tip)
INCIDENCE:	3 degrees, 30 minutes *(B-26B-1 and C-models)*
	7 degrees *(B-26F and B-26G models)*
DIHEDRAL:	1 degree, 17 minutes (measured at the leading edge)
WING AREA (less ailerons):	613.3 sq. ft.
AILERON AREA (total):	44.7 sq. ft.
FLAPS (total):	71.82 sq. ft.

Stabilizer data:

SPAN:	28 ft., 0 in.
INCIDENCE:	Minus 30 minutes
DIHEDRAL:	8 degrees
AREA (including elevators):	160.2 sq. ft.

Vertical fin and rudder data:

RUDDER AREA (including tab):

Long chord:	43.887 sq. ft.
Short chord:	40.026 sq. ft.

(Long chord rudders were used on B-26B-1 aircraft 41-18185 – 18334, 41-31573 – 31672, and B-26C aircraft 41-34673 – 35372. They had a travel of 25 degrees, 21.44 inches either side of center. Short chord rudders were used on B-26B-1 41-31673, B-26C 41-35373, and all subsequent Marauders. They had a travel of 25 degrees, 18.94 inches, according to the manual.)

Fuselage data:

WIDTH (maximum):	7 ft., 8 in.
HEIGHT (maximum):	7 ft., 10.5 in.

Landing gear data:

MAIN GEAR:	Hydraulically retractable.
MAIN GEAR TREAD:	21 ft., 11 in. (from center of tire to center of tire).
MAIN WHEELS:	Goodyear 17:00-20 low pressure, 530397.
MAIN TIRES:	17:00-20 low pressure.
NOSE GEAR:	Hydraulically retractable.
NOSE WHEEL:	33 in. smooth contour.
NOSE TIRE:	33 in. smooth contour.

Engine data:

TYPE:	Pratt & Whitney R-2800-43 (2,000 hp).
GEAR RATIO:	1:0.500 (2:1).
FUEL:	AN-F-28, Grade 130.
OIL:	AN-VV-O-446, Grade 1120.

Propeller data:

MANUFACTURER:	Curtiss or Lycoming (blades only).
TYPE:	Four-blade, electrically controlled, full-feathering.
HUB NUMBER:	108049 (including brush assembly).
BLADE NUMBER:	Curtiss design 814-2C3-18.
	Lycoming design C3821306.
PROPELLER DIAMETER:	13 ft., 6 in.
PITCH SETTING:	Low (fine): 17 degrees; High (coarse): 47 degrees.

Tank capacities:

MAIN WING TANKS (2):	B-26B-1 and B-26C, 360 U.S. gal.; 300 Imperial gal.
	B-26F and B-26G, 380 U.S. gal.; 316 Imperial gal.
AUXILIARY WING TANKS (2):	121 U.S. gal.; 100 Imperial gal.
TOTAL:	B-26B-1 and B-26C, 481 U.S. gal.; 400 Imperial gal.
	B-26F and B-26G, 501 U.S. gal.; 417 Imperial gal.
FORWARD BOMB BAY:	Metal type, 250 U.S. gal.; 208 Imperial gal.
	Self-sealing type, 268 U.S. gal.; 223 Imperial gal.
OIL TANK (1 per engine):	41.25 U.S. gal.; 34.33 Imperial gal.

Performance (from various sources):

MODEL	CRUISE	TOP SPEED	RANGE
B-26C-5	214 mph	282 mph at 15,000 ft.	1,150 mi. with 3,000 lbs. of bombs
B-26G	216 mph	283 mph at 5,000 ft.	1,100 mi. with 4,000 lbs. of bombs
		274 mph at 15,000 ft.	

SIGNIFICANT DATES

11 March 1939: Invitation for bids invited by Circular Proposal 39-640 led to creation of the Martin B-26 Marauder twin engine bomber.

20 September 1939: Assistant Secretary of War approved Gen. H. H. Arnold's recommendation to order 201 Martin Model 179 (B-26) bombers for $16,029,750; additional engineering aspects added nearly $100,000 to this initial amount.

29 November 1940: First flight of the B-26 Marauder.

8 February 1941: First B-26 of contract No. ac-13243 accepted from Martin.

12 April 1942: Directive issued to turn over many B-26 and B-26A variants to AAF schools for instructional purposes. Directives in May and June 1942 provided for modification of all straight B-26 and B-26A aircraft for gunnery training duties.

4 June 1942: Four torpedo-wielding B-26s attacked the Japanese fleet near Midway.

12 November 1942: Bad weather compounded navigation problems that led a ferry flight of 319th Bomb Group B-26s from southern England over Cherbourg as they strove to head toward North Africa. This first inadvertent Marauder foray over the Continent saw two B-26s shot down and a third damaged and forced to crash land back at Warmwell in England.

28 November 1942: Official operational debut of 12th Air Force B-26s came with a 319th Bomb Group Marauder strike over Sfax.

17 May 1943: Eighth Air Force Marauder minimum altitude mission over Holland ended in disaster when all 10 B-26s to reach the Continent were destroyed; Eighth Air Force halted further low-level Marauder operations.

16 October 1943: European Theater of Operations B-26s (322nd, 323rd, 386th, and 387th Bomb Groups) transferred to Ninth Air Force from Eighth Air Force.

9 August 1944: Pilot Capt. Darrell R. Lindsey of 394th Bomb Group earned Medal of Honor for staying with his stricken Marauder to afford rest of crew time to bail out.

22 February 1945: First resumption of low-level missions for B-26s in the European Theater of Operations since 1943.

30 March 1945: End of Marauder production; last aircraft was a TB-26G.

1948: U.S. Air Force declared Marauders obsolete; few remained in Air Force service.

April 1972: B-26 40-1464 and two others arrived at Chino, California, for restoration under the auspices of collector David Tallichet.

18 April 1992: First post-rebuilding flight of B-26 40-1464 after recovery from Canadian wilderness.

Members of the 8th Tow Target Squadron posed with Mortimer, an AT-23 used by the squadron at McChord Field, near Tacoma, Washington, circa 1943-44. (AFHRA)